This book is smartly written, scripturally sound, and quite frankly . . . captivating. Connie tackles deep theological issues with ease and insight. Coping with pain and suffering, while embracing an all-loving and all-powerful God has been with Christianity from the beginning, but she shows an ability to make deep spiritual truths much less difficult to grasp. There is freedom in her words that echo with the Word of God. I could not recommend this book more.

Jimmy Myers, Ph.D., LPC-S, CSAT
CEO of The Timothy Center & Author

Why would we need faith if we never felt the urge to question it? In this uplifting masterpiece, Connie Hagen addresses the probing, faith-testing questions we tend to ask ourselves through life's difficult transitions. She clarifies for us, once and for all, how we should think of God in relation to our circumstances. As an integrative cancer physician with over thirty years of experience, I have been a personal witness to the journey of thousands of late-stage cancer patients. Common to most of them has been the question, "Why?" To help our patients find their answers, we have brought our ministry to them, helping them find hope as they seek faith in the darkest of times. I can assure you, from here forth, I will recommend this book to every one of them who asks me their unanswerable question. And in moments when I feel my own faith challenged, I will be sure to pick it up and read it for myself once again.

Antonio "Tony" Jimenez, M.D., N.D.
Founder and Chief Medical Officer
Hope4Cancer Treatment Centers

Have you been served a cup you want the Lord to take from you, or maybe you don't understand why it's been given to you? Connie's captivating, relatable, and raw stories are intertwined with powerful lessons. The Lord will speak to you from these pages. Freedom and healing will be delivered through her wise, God-given words."

Katie Novickas, M.Ed.
Children's Director, Life Dripping Springs

Drinking the Cup You are Served is a divine appointment. Connie's personal life stories, written among the pages of this book, are a testament to the faithfulness of the Lord. Within each chapter she generously shares engaging truths that not only give your pain a voice, but it raises the level of your awareness to manage life's challenges head-on while also providing activation tools prayerfully chosen to assist you during this season. Regardless of current or past challenges, heartaches, or obstacles, Connie's book will serve as a trusted guide to come back to during life's unexpected challenges.

Deana L. Morgan
Teacher, Speaker, Consultant
Author of *From the Symptoms to the Secret*

Drinking The Cup You Are Served was a book I could not put down. When I finished one chapter, I wanted to go on to the next. Connie's personal stories of the cups she has had to drink were compelling. When your read this book, you will have a front-row seat into not only her life but the lives of various characters in the Bible who have also had to drink a bitter cup. Connie shares these stories with such candor and ease. In the pages of this book, you will come to understand who God is in the midst of your brokenness and grief and realize the presence of God is always the best place to find shelter in whatever painful circumstance you may encounter. Connie also masterfully integrates psychological principles and tools to help you navigate your thoughts and emotions through the unexpected and the unwanted. I hope you enjoy this book as much as I have.

Mike D. Robertson, M.Div.
Author of *Dealing with Difficult People*

In this book Connie Hagen sits with us as we drink the cup we wish we didn't have to drink. With honesty, compassion, and incredible skill, she equips us to face unexpected heartache with the wisdom of a therapist and the understanding of a woman who has been there. Providing practical tools and deep insight, *Drinking the Cup You Are Served* is an essential resource to the world of mental and emotional health. Thank you, Connie, for pouring your heart into these pages so you might be a guiding light for those who feel the darkness closing in.

Jennifer Strickland
Author, *Girl Perfect and Beautiful Lies*
TEDx speaker, and founder of URMore.org.

Drinking the Cup You Are Served is a treasure you never realized you were looking for. In this book you will find a little of yourself and others you know through the stories Connie Hagen weaves through her examples of real-life experiences people have faced. She even describes biblical characters who have faced similar experiences. As you read you will begin to understand why you perceive or react to certain circumstances in your life the way you do, maybe even differently than others. This is the kind of book you can turn to again and again. I have already used this book to help counsel someone because of the insight the book has given me. It is an enjoyable, thought-provoking, insightful read full of the Word of God as its foundation. Don't miss it!

Jenny Juhl
Assistant Director
Christ for the Nations, Fellowship of Ministries and Churches

If life has ever hit you so hard the room is spinning, you need to read this book. Connie shares from a lifetime of walking beside the hurt and confusion, while reaching into the painful places of her own story to reveal the beauty and grace found in the most bitter cups life can serve.

Brock Stamps
Pastor, LifeDripping Springs

Drinking The Cup You Are Served is for those who need hope and perspective during extremely challenging times. It is for those who want to know how to be a better friend and guide to those around them. What you will experience in this wonderful book is, as if Connie had invited you into her home, poured you a cup of coffee, and then taken the time to share wise and scripture-filled counsel from a loving transparent confidante.

RT Phillips
Former President of Promise Keepers
Pastor and Ministry Leader

As spiritual leaders God has called us to be dealers of hope for people who are suffering the ill-effects of a fallen, broken world cursed by sin. Fortunately, we now have a valuable resource to help all of us, regardless of our station in life. In this book Connie combines her valuable experience as a licensed professional therapist with her life-long journey walking out her faith commitment to Jesus Christ. With a creative nexus of biblical truth and psychological principles, Connie features familiar characters in the Bible who struggled with the same common issues that plague so many of us today. Then she integrates practical cognitive behavior skills with proven principles from Scripture to help her readers face their own circumstances with courageous faith. Spiritual freedom and emotional healing are God's desire for each one of us, and Connie points the way with such refreshing insight and clarity. *Drinking the Cup You are Served* needs to be a reference tool in the library of every spiritual leader as we are so often called upon to serve those who feel overwhelmed by the hurts of life.

Mark & Pam Morrow
Founding Pastors, CrossWalk Church
Williamsburg, Virginia

Drinking the Cup You Are Served

Living Beyond Your Circumstances

Connie Hagen, M.Ed.

CREATIVE ENTERPRISES STUDIO

BEDFORD, TEXAS

Published by Books, Bach & Beyond, Inc. d/b/a Creative Enterprises Studio, 1507 Shirley Way, Suite A, Bedford, TX 76022. CreativeEnterprisesStudio.com.

Unless otherwise noted, Scripture quotations are taken from the Holy Bible, New International Version®, NIV®. Copyright © 1973, 1978, 1984, 2011 by Biblica, Inc.™ Used by permission of Zondervan. All rights reserved worldwide. www.zondervan.com. The "NIV" and "New International Version" are trademarks registered in the United States Patent and Trademark Office by Biblica, Inc.™

Scripture quotations marked ESV are from the ESV® Bible (The Holy Bible, English Standard Version®), copyright © 2001 by Crossway, a publishing ministry of Good News Publishers. Used by permission. All rights reserved.

Scripture quotations marked KJV are from the King James Version. Public domain.

Scripture quotations marked THE MESSAGE are from The Message. Copyright © 1993, 2002, 2018 by Eugene H. Peterson. Used by permission of NavPress. All rights reserved. Represented by Tyndale House Publishers, a division of Tyndale House Ministries.

Scripture quotations marked NLT are from the *Holy Bible*, New Living Translation. © 1996, 2004, 2015 by Tyndale House Foundation. Used by permission of Tyndale House Ministries, Carol Stream, Illinois 60188. All rights reserved.

Scripture quotations marked NRSV are from the New Revised Standard Version Bible. Copyright © 1989 National Council of the Churches of Christ in the United States of America. Used by permission. All rights reserved worldwide.

"BLESSING IN THE THORN." Words and Music by Randy Phillips, Koch, Don and Dave Clark. © 1997 Curb Word Music (ASCAP) and Curb Dayspring Music (BMI). All rights on behalf of Curb Word Music administered by WC Music Corp. All rights on behalf of Curb Dayspring Music administered by Warner-Tamerlane Publishing Corp.

Library of Congress Control Number: 2022912883

Softcover ISBN: 979-8-9857329-6-2
E-Book ISBN: 979-8-9857329-7-9
Cover Design: StudioAnneli.com

Printed in the United States of America
22 23 24 25 26 27   MG   6 5 4 3 2 1

This book is dedicated to my family.

To my husband:
Your faith in me gave me wings.

To my children:
Your encouragement enabled me to fly. You lifted me, challenged me,
and inspired me to offer this work as a gift to those drinking the cup
of suffering.

To my parents:
I am who I am because of you.

Contents

Part One: *Setting the Table*

Part Two: *Drinking the Cup*

Foreword

$\mathcal{J}$esus was offered a cup full of humanities' brokenness. That cup, metaphorically, represented a reduction syrup of sin and shame which began in the first garden with our first parents. In this garden of God's divine will, Jesus struggled to drink the cup. Think about that for a moment…Jesus struggled to drink the cup He was served. If Jesus struggled, where does that leave us? Perfectly in God's gracious hands.

Connie Hagen has been a long-time member of my church in Austin, Texas. She and her precious family have helped grow our church and plant new churches in Central Texas. Besides being brilliant, competent, and compassionate, Connie is an incredibly gifted leader in our church. I am so proud of her book, *Drinking the Cup You are Served*. Well done, Connie.

Each vowel and consonant of her book is bathed in the experiences of her life and is an outflow of her heart of grace. *Drinking the Cup You are Served* will equip and empower you to hold your cup, face your circumstances, change your perception, and accept what life has brought you as a gift to bring transformation to your own life.

"Never change" was written in my yearbook by at least a dozen people. Obviously, that's the worst advice I've ever received. We are supposed to be constantly changing into kinder, humbler, more faithful expressions of who we were created to be. Change and growth occur most often when we are pressed by the extreme highs and lows of life. Connie pulls back the curtain of her own life and allows us to see the scars, the wounds, and the way she has overcome. Her practical and spiritual insights will help your heart to heal and soften the edges that have become shattered by the unexpected circumstances in your life.

God offers us a cup—that difficult and sometimes unbearable circumstance—that impacts you relationally, financially, spiritually, or physically.

Following in the steps of Jesus, we can resist the temptation to reject it (Jesus did three times), or we can choose to ingest it (Jesus did after prayer). God is committed to walking alongside us during our times of sorrow and pain. He wants to transform you as he transformed Christ that night in the garden.

Let me tell you, God is crazy about you and the shape of your heart. He is not frowning or disappointed when he thinks of you. "He makes His face to shine upon you" (Numbers 6:24). He intentionally looks at you with great hope and favor. You have his undivided attention. Now, drink the cup, knowing your Father's gracious hands are holding it.

To the reader, lean into the deep water of Connie's masterpiece and watch God do the miracle only he can do.

Randy Phillips,
Lead Pastor Life.Family
Founder of Phillips, Craig and Dean

Introduction
Because Life Can Change in a Flash

$\mathcal{O}$ne July afternoon, I sank into my favorite rocking chair on the front porch with an icy glass of lemonade. It's always hot in July in the small town of Bastrop, Texas. Today felt especially so because I was tired. I'd been running all morning, working on office matters for my husband's medical practice, going over some homeschooling work with our kids, keeping our corner of the world together as best I could. I looked forward to some peace and quiet—a pause.

Then, just as I took that first sip of cool lemonade, the phone rang. My neighbor's daughter-in-law, who had given birth to their second child only five days earlier, was in the intensive care unit of a hospital in Austin. Carrie had been flown there the night before by CareFlight, an emergency medical helicopter. The medical team diagnosed her with sepsis, a whole-body inflammation caused by a serious staph infection. She was only semi-conscious and not expected to live.

Not expected to live? I set down my glass. The beautiful afternoon, the busy morning, the tiredness I felt—all the things of an ordinary day melted away. Our world suddenly turned upside down, as if that refreshing glass of lemonade had dropped, spilled, shattered, and left a broken, sticky mess.

I rushed to my neighbor's house and promised to watch Carrie's oldest daughter, Amy, who had been staying with her grandmother through the ordeal. Before stepping into their home, I took a deep breath, thinking, *What can I possibly say to comfort a seven-year-old girl who is about to lose her mother?* Nothing.

Without a word, I scooped up Amy in my arms and hugged her tight. "I'll be here," I assured, "as long as you need me." Amy was my daughter's age, and they were playmates, and my heart was broken for her and my neighbor and friends. I brought her home with me. She ran to play with my daughter, which was the most comforting thing at the moment for both her and me. It appeared normal, and I wanted everything to feel as normal as they had been and could be again. When dinnertime came, I prepared supper and we ate. At bedtime, I helped Amy get ready and tucked her in with a kiss on her forehead.

But things were not as they had been. Amy asked if I would lay down with her and hold her hand until she fell asleep.

In that moment, I knew Amy had a strong sense something terrible was going to happen to her mother, and I was the one God had chosen to be with her through this. I also knew she counted on me to reach out and offer her a mother's touch, which was something I could do.

I slipped into bed with Amy and my daughter, and we all held hands as they both curled into me. I prayed out loud for Jesus to heal Amy's mother and bring us peace. It was a simple prayer; all I could pray . . . and all that we needed at that moment.

Morning came. Amy rose and approached me with the tenderness that only a child can possess. She looked me straight in the eye and asked, "Is my mother going to die?"

All evening and through the night, I had known this question was coming, but how could I tell this innocent child such a hard, ugly truth? How could I tell of a loss that I know would forever change her life?

Knowing Amy would carefully measure the weight of every word, I took a deep breath. "Your mom is very sick," I began, "but she is fighting to stay alive. We are praying God will heal her."

Amy looked at me for what seemed like an eternity, then asked when she could see her mother.

This wasn't the response I expected. "I don't know," I stammered, "but I hope soon."

With that, she went to play again with my daughter, and I sat quiet and still to pray for what we all hoped: to see one another soon, to have life go back to the way it had been, all that was familiar and right and good.

But this was not to be.

Amy stayed with us four days until her mother lost her fight and passed away the morning of my birthday. Every one of those four nights, I took Amy's hand and lay next to her until she drifted into sleep, praying God would cover her with his comfort and peace.

In a moment, the worst happened, and life changed irrevocably. A little girl and a newborn baby lost their mother; a husband lost his wife; a mother lost her daughter; a neighbor lost a friend.

Bad things happen in this world, and no one is immune: not a neighbor, not little children, not you or me trying to get through an ordinary day. The ordinary, in fact, can change in an instant. The beauty, the peace and quiet or refreshment we seek in this life can be spilled and shattered.

And so here we are, in different circumstances than we ever wanted or wished for and maybe feared. Someone you love can die, or you find yourself in the middle of a divorce you never wanted—or maybe you did want it because you were in agony, but now you feel utterly alone and abandoned because you've lost not just a spouse but a circle of friends, a way of life. Or maybe you lost your job and an income, or your home or your health. The list of circumstances that were never wanted can go on and on, as wide as this earth, as long as the ages.

How do you go on?

Introduction

Just as there were steps to take to go to my friend in need, I've found there are steps we can take to live fully and freely again beyond any terrible circumstance. There are things you can do to go forward. There is refreshment for your thirsty soul, and nourishment and comfort for your shattered heart. There are prayers. There is hope.

After Amy lost her mother, I took her a gift basket. We do this, don't we? We cook in the midst of our grief. We give gifts. We look for ways to show those in their time of heartache that we are thinking of them and care. In some way, we want to be present with them and there for them through all that is difficult ahead. So into this basket, I tucked two china cups, soothing tea, homemade banana bread, a journal, a pillow pet, and a locket with a picture of her mother inside. All these little things I wanted to add up to show Amy that she was not alone. I wanted her to know that whatever cup life serves her, there would be someone there to take it all in with her.

It is my prayer for you to find the same gifts in these pages. Whatever cup life has served you, I want you to know you can take that cup, own it, sit with it, drink from it, and move forward. You'll find acknowledgment of your pain, whatever the situation, and food for your soul in the truth of God's promises. There are tools for your mind, body, and spirit, and when life serves you painful circumstances, you can overcome them through the transforming power of Christ. This book will walk you through steps and help you find peace and hope. Together, we will look at what to do when life gives you what feels like too much and tastes too awful to swallow. You will discover there is a way to get back to the front porch of your life, to find hope and purpose again, because each extraordinary day is a gift. You will come to understand God is the one who restores your soul. He is the light in your darkness. He will sit with you in your pain and help you find a way to move forward again.

"Going a little farther, he fell with his face to the ground and prayed, 'My Father, if it is possible, may this cup be taken from me. Yet not as I will, but as you will.'"

Matthew 26:39

Part One

Setting the Table

1
I Don't Want to Drink this Cup
How to Face Your Circumstances

*S*o what's really going on—how are you doing?"

This very question drew my friend Lisa to tears. She was visiting during the holiday season. We have been celebrating together since we were twentysomethings living in Dallas, where we met and formed a close-knit group we affectionately called the Fabulous Five. We were all so close. For twenty years, we'd shared everything about our lives. But over the last two years she'd become increasingly distant, almost aloof. I realized on this particular day I'd been doing most of the talking, sharing about things going on with my family, but Lisa hadn't shared anything. She would either listen to me silently or change the subject to surface-level things. Our conversation wasn't really a conversation. She had withdrawn, keeping me at arm's length. I felt shut out. Our friendship, once so deep, had become shallow.

Over the last seven years, I'd seen pieces of Lisa dropping away. She was once a dynamic Bible teacher who was actively involved in her church. One of the first things that had drawn me to her was her passion for God, along with her gifted way of teaching Bible studies and speaking to crowds at women's ministry events and groups. Now she wasn't doing any speaking or teaching. She went to church only sporadically.

Lisa had married a man who didn't share her same love for Christ. She thought her husband might find faith during their marriage, but they were driven by different things. They struggled. The two of them tried starting a family, thinking that would bring them closer. Then

Lisa suffered an ectopic pregnancy, where the baby develops outside the uterus. She had to go through surgery, and she lost her unborn child.

My dear friend was devastated. She couldn't conceive again because of what her body had gone through, so she and her husband decided to adopt. They found a precious baby girl, brought her home, and instantly fell in love with her. Three weeks later, the birth mother changed her mind and took the baby away.

Something in Lisa broke. She checked out emotionally. Her husband checked out too. He eventually had an affair, and their marriage ended in divorce.

Single again, Lisa threw herself into her career. She was offered an upper-management position at a large bank and switched jobs from the company where she'd worked the last ten years. She labored longer and harder as an executive, but the new job wasn't what she expected. No job, she realized, was going to fill the empty places.

This is when she stopped going to church. She cut herself off from church friends, our circle of friends from the early Dallas days, and me too.

When I relentlessly nudged her to open up, she finally broke down. She admitted she'd lost the essence of who she was, that all her passion and purpose had gotten lost in so much pain.

"If it weren't for Winnie, I don't know what I'd do," she said between tears. Her little terrier was all she had left of the family she had hoped for, dreamed of, and tried to build. Her life had become this meaningless cycle of dragging herself out of bed to a job that was taking everything out of her, only to return home, then drag herself out of bed the next morning to start it all over again. "My life isn't at all what I expected," she said, wiping her tears with a Kleenex. "I'm single. Alone. All I do is work in a job that is sucking the life from me. I have nothing to show for my life."

She laughed. "I guess, putting it that way, if you cannot be a good example, at least be a terrible warning."

She was only half-joking. My heart broke for her.

As we talked about her depression, she became vulnerable and confessed hopelessness. In that moment of honesty and vulnerability, I saw a glimmer of the old Lisa flicker. She said, almost as much to herself as to me, that she didn't blame God and wasn't mad at him for the series of sad events in her life. She blamed herself. "I'm the one who made all these choices—about my husband, my job, checking out."

In the midst of our discussion, she was determined to find her way back to living with purpose—on purpose again.

Yes, I prayed silently. *This is the Lisa I know and love.*

In the weeks and months following, Lisa did make her way back, picking up piece by piece of herself. She began to rediscover her purpose along the way. We talked more often. She found a new church and made a new friend in the pastor's wife. She began surrounding herself with friends and a spiritual family. She started doing things again, going places, getting involved, engaging in life.

Then one evening I got a text message from one of our mutual friends: "Call me as soon as you can."

I called and learned that a stray dog had broken through Lisa's backyard fence and attacked Winnie.

"Winnie's dead."

I arranged the drive from Austin to Dallas to go to Lisa as quickly as possible. The evening before I left, I learned the details of Winnie's death. Lisa had let Winnie into the backyard, then vacuumed the house. When she opened the door to call Winnie back inside, she saw a little heap near the back fence and a gaping hole, as if someone had hacked their way into the yard. Lisa ran to Winnie, who lay crumpled, bloody, and still. She had never heard her old dog's cries over the hum of the vacuum and never saw the stray that had attacked Winnie. Lisa scooped her little dog to her chest, raced to her car, and sped to the vet's office.

Nothing could save Winnie. Having been shaken too hard by the stray, she had lost too much blood and her little body was in shreds. Before Lisa could fully comprehend what had happened, her sole companion was gone.

She drove to her mother's house in tears.

By the time I got there, Lisa was numb. She greeted me at the door, looking emptier than anyone I had ever seen. I hugged her tight, but she couldn't soften and didn't break down. She was spent.

We sat in the living room, making small talk. Every attempt seemed awkward and hard. Finally, we didn't try. Talking took too much effort. "I'm sorry" and "I'm so sad" are too inadequate of words after such loss upon loss.

The next morning, I drove Lisa to the veterinary office to collect Winnie's remains. She sat in the passenger seat, Winnie's collar, the blood-stained blanket, and a container of ashes in her lap. Though Lisa was within arm's reach, she seemed so far away. Limp. Hollow. Helpless.

"I have nothing to show for my life . . . nothing . . . If you cannot be a good example, at least be a terrible warning." Lisa's words from that Christmas came back to me. It was as if I heard her speak them out loud again, but when I glanced sideways at her, Lisa stared ahead vacantly.

She is gone, I thought. I began to pray silently. *Why, God? Just when she was finding her way back. Why?*

Only this time, there was no going back. In the days and weeks following the brutal attack that killed Winnie, Lisa checked out completely. The thought of going back to her own home was too devastating for her, so she moved in with her mother. She stayed home from work for days. When she did go back to work, she was perfunctory about it. She did her job, came home, went to bed, and pulled the covers over her head. The steps she had made toward finding her way back had been reversed. She would not reach out to her closest friends for comfort and support; she retreated. Lisa had lost her purpose to live fully every day.

The question that hovered over her thoughts and ours was, *Why?*

But none of us—not her friends, not people of counsel—had any answers.

ASKING THE UNANSWERABLE WHY?

"Why?" is the question everyone asks when something terrible happens. It's the natural question when things don't make sense after you've lost someone or something you love, whether it's a person, a friendship, a job, a home, your health, or a dream. It's the question you can't help but dwell on when you ache so deeply there are no words—only a sob and a cry. *Why?*

It's the question that brings people to me with the hope that I can help them find answers. But how do you answer the unanswerable?

The Scriptures say time and chance happen to everyone (Ecclesiastes 9:11). Sometimes the little you know is all there is. A friend dies. A child gets leukemia. Out of nowhere comes a tragedy. *Why?* There are no answers.

I learned this profoundly when, as a young therapist, I worked with women who had been abused as children. They wanted to know how someone who was supposed to love them, care for them, and protect them could hurt them over and over again. *Why?*

I couldn't say. I didn't know. Not any more than I knew why a little girl's mother was taken away by a terrible illness, or why a baby must die before being born, or why my dearest friend Lisa suffered loss after terrible loss.

All I know is life just happens. There is an incident or an accident, and something terrible occurs. Things go wrong. People are hurt, and hearts get broken. Life as you know it stops. You get knocked to the ground, and you don't know how to get up or even if you want to.

You think getting answers will relieve your pain and bring you comfort. You think it will help you make sense of everything. You tell yourself: *If I just understand why then I won't hurt so badly. I'll deal with everything better. If I just know the reason this happened, I'll keep myself from going through it again.*

"But to have no reason for it all?" one woman asked me once. "How do you accept that?"

How do you accept it? The desperation to know why and the lack of answers can surely turn you inside out and spin you in circles. When there are no answers, you can feel lost in the dark, empty and hopeless, like there's nothing left for you in this world. Or like Lisa, you can live on autopilot, moving through life passionless and numb, as if the light has gradually faded into darkness.

Wanting to know why can be incredibly seducing. It's a question that entices you into believing its answer will somehow give you peace, satisfaction, and the sense of control you think you desperately need to feel better. But more often than not there is no good answer, and we are left feeling empty and betrayed. Not every why is unanswerable, but when it demands an answer, it will lead you down a path to further heartache and spin you into a deeper web of despair.

Asking the unanswerable why landed Lisa in a place of desperation. She became lost to herself and us. This was her dark night of the soul. However, while asking why wasn't helping her, it wasn't any reason for shame. As Lisa would put it later, "Why can't I ask why? Even Jesus Christ did."

IT'S ONLY HUMAN TO ASK WHY

It's true. Jesus, both fully human and fully divine, asked why. When he hung on the cross, he begged God to answer this haunting question: "'My God, my God, why have you forsaken me?'" (Matthew 27:46).

Didn't Jesus have every reason to ask his Father why, after everything he'd given up, after doing all God had asked him to do? Hadn't he suffered enough already? His friends had scattered. Judas had betrayed him outright, and the others had denied him under pressure. His ministry had been turned inside out. Even his clothes had been stripped away, divided among his torturers. And now his Father turned away as well?

Why?

What a clear snapshot into suffering. In the garden of Gethsemane, the night before he hung on the cross, Jesus desperately cried out to his Father, asking him why. He bared his soul as a son, a man, a human. He was honest with God and transparent with everyone around him. "If this cup could be passed," he prayed, "God, do it. Take it. Take it away." There was only silence. There were no answers.

In this lonely, hard, agonizing place, Jesus gave us an example of what to do. He showed us it really is okay to ask why, to wrestle in our dark night, our own garden of Gethsemane where we feel betrayed by life. Then, once there is no answer, when there is still only mystery, only silence, we need to let go. It makes no sense to stay there demanding an answer that will never come—asking why didn't keep Christ from the cross. It wouldn't save Lisa from despair either. Continuing to ask why isn't going to get you through the agony that life often serves.

If anything, life is a storm of things: waves of joy and hurt. There are gifts, and there is loss. Everything costs something, and the cost often involves suffering. You enter suffering like a small boat in an uncharted ocean with a storm brewing in the distance. In what feels like a moment, the storm hits your tiny boat with violent waves of confusion and anguish. You are suddenly thrown about and there's nothing steady for you to hold on to. You're terrified of being swallowed into the black, yawning depths. You fear not making it out alive.

The last thing you need in this moment is a lesson on meteorology; knowing why the storm rages doesn't remove you from it. Asking why you're suffering won't give you something to hang on to or get you through the blinding spray. It won't stop the fierce battering of the waves or the ocean depths of depression, anger, frustration, or fear. Knowing why won't diminish the hurt, despair, and distress of your tragedy and loss.

In the same way, you don't need theories on why a storm is happening in a relationship or a situation to get through it. You don't need a lesson on theology during times of tragedy, hurt, and sorrow, and scriptures quoted at you won't stop you from feeling what you feel. Platitudes won't make everything fine. Neither will personal opinions on why things happened the way they did. Knowing why won't change the bad to good. And most importantly, continuing to ask why will not stop the storm you're in; instead, it may have the opposite effect. Remaining fixed upon the why can keep you in it, take you back to it, and eventually undo you.

ASKING THE RIGHT QUESTION

In the midst of Lisa's storm, when she and all of us who loved her were asking why, I had to step back a minute and think of what I say when so many of my hurting and despondent clients come to me with the same question. "Why hasn't God saved me from this? Why hasn't he stepped in?"

Why, I remembered, isn't the right question. Asking why doesn't get you anywhere.

However, asking the question *What do I believe?* does. Knowing what you believe gives you a way of steadying yourself in the storm. Knowing God is fundamentally good—that he loves you, that he will be with you and ultimately save you, gives you hope—but not knowing who he is and what he is able to do leaves you feeling alone and hopeless.

Knowing what you believe is like having an anchor. You can tether yourself sound and secure to the promises of God, believing he is good, he does love you, and he will stay by you in every storm. He promises to guide you and bring you ashore and put you back onto dry land. These assurances will anchor you and keep you from drifting. They are the grounding truths you can stand upon amid a terrible circumstance. They will stabilize you in the middle of a terrifying storm and help you discover hope in the aftermath. They are the promises that will keep you from flailing, give you courage, steady your course, and keep your light burning.

When clients I've worked with could answer the question, "What do I believe?" they were able to see through the fog and blasting waves of loss, pain, and despair. They could act on their beliefs, exercise faith in them, and experience the courage, strength, and peace that faith produces in us. They did not just *say* they believed; they acted and *exercised* their faith that God would stay by them, somehow work things for good, and get them through it all.

But my clients who were fixed on "why?" couldn't see past anything. They were stuck on why they were in the boat, why the ocean was so big, why they had been caught in such a bad storm, why God would let this happen—*why, why, why?*

This is where it's good to stop and ask yourself, "What do I really believe?" It's okay if you don't yet know. You can begin by looking through the lens of Jesus Christ to see God from his perspective. Ask yourself, "What did Jesus know and understand about God that helped him drink the cup those unbearable days, through the garden, the cross, and the grave?" I believe Jesus understood fully the character of God. He knew who his Father was—his Father was the same yesterday, today, and forever regardless of the circumstance. He understood his Father saw the bigger picture, and Jesus trusted him wholeheartedly. That night in the garden, Jesus was able to surrender his will because he trusted his Father could see what he couldn't. He knew God had a bigger plan, and he understood his Father's plan was intended to bring forth good things. His beliefs about the nature of his Father gave Jesus the courage to drink from that bitter cup

WHO IS GOD?

Knowing and understanding the character and nature of God is essential when walking through unexpected tragedy, trauma, and heartache. Let's take a moment to look at the attributes of God, the very beliefs that Jesus held on to during the cross.

God Is Loving

God loves us so much he sent his only Son to die on the cross for the redemption of our sin. His love for us is more powerful than death and stronger than the grave. God knit us together in our mother's womb, which means he loved us even before we were born. In Jeremiah 31:3 God said, "I have loved you with an everlasting love," and in Romans 8:38–39, we learn "I am convinced that nothing can ever separate us from God's love. Neither death nor life, neither angels nor demons, neither our fears for today nor our worries about tomorrow—not even the powers of hell can separate us from God's love. No power in the sky above or in the earth below—indeed, nothing in all creation will ever be able to separate us from the love of God that is revealed in Christ Jesus our Lord" (NLT). God's love is unconditional, is everlasting, and endures forever.

God Is Our Comforter

God comforts us in times of sorrow, fear, dread, and indecision. He is there when we feel anxious and uncertain. He is our strong tower, our refuge and place of rest, the comfort for our souls. In 2 Corinthians 1:3–4, Paul said, "Praise be to the God and Father of our Lord Jesus Christ, the Father of compassion and the God of all comfort, who comforts us in all our troubles." God lifts our burdens and helps us let go of our affliction. Jesus calls out to us, saying, "Come to me, all you who are weary and burdened, and I will give you rest. Take my yoke upon you and learn from me, for I am gentle and humble in heart, and you will find rest for your souls. For my yoke is easy and my burden is light" (Matthew 11:28–30).

God Is Faithful

God is the same yesterday, today, and forever. He doesn't change who he is or what he has promised. He is constant and true even when we are not. Jeremiah proclaimed in Lamentations 3:22–23 that God's faithfulness is new every day: "The steadfast love of the LORD never ceases; his mercies never come to an end; they are new every morning; great is your faithfulness" (ESV). David expressed repeatedly in the Psalms that God abounds in love and faithfulness. He is forever with us and for us.

God Is Merciful

God is a God of tender hearted compassion toward all of us. His mercy is so great he sacrificed his only Son so we could have eternal life with him. There is nothing we can do to merit such mercy. It is a gift he has freely given to us. Jesus shed his blood so we could be cleansed and made whole. When we are forgiven, we are able to enter into the presence of God without shame or blemish. Christ's shed blood has purified us. God's mercy and unfailing love are what sustains us. In Lamentations 3:31–33, we read, "The Master won't ever walk out and fail to return. If he works severely, he also works tenderly. His stockpiles of loyal love are immense. He takes no pleasure in making life hard, in throwing roadblocks in the way (THE MESSAGE). Psalm 86:15 says, "But you, O Lord, are a God merciful and gracious, slow to anger and abounding in steadfast love and faithfulness" (ESV). Though we struggle in this life, God reveals his tender mercies every day.

God Is Holy

The very nature of God is holy, making him pure and perfect. He is so holy that his presence lights the heavens, shakes the temple, and fills our world with his glory. Even the angels in heaven cry out, "Holy, holy,

holy" (Isaiah 6:3). God is perfect, without sin—there is no evil in him. We are told in 1 Samuel 2:2, "There is none holy like the LORD; for there is none besides you; there is no rock like our God" (ESV). Isaiah 6:3 says, "Holy, holy, holy is the LORD of hosts; the whole earth is full of his glory!" (ESV). Regardless of what happens in our world today, God remains holy!

God Is All-Powerful

Nothing and no one are beyond God; nothing can overpower him. He made the earth with his power, established the world with his wisdom, and stretched out the heavens by his understanding. Colossians 1:16 says, "For by him all things were created, in heaven and on earth, visible and invisible, whether thrones or dominions or rulers or authorities— all things were created through him and for him" (ESV). Because we live in a fallen world, tragedy and heartache happen. Still, in the midst of our suffering, God's power gets us through our grief. God cares so deeply for us he will fight on our behalf to give us supernatural strength and courage to walk through our heartbreak and sorrow.

God Is Our Healer

God is the one who heals our brokenness. In the Old Testament, God is referred to as Jehovah Rapha, our healer. He is the one who heals our emotional, physical, and spiritual brokenness. God promised from the beginning, "I am the LORD, who heals you" (Exodus 15:26). There are many examples in the Bible where God restored sight to the blind and hearing to the deaf. He enabled the crippled man to walk, and he caused the mute to speak and the dead to live again. When you are hurting, you can turn to him to make you whole, mend your wounds, and restore your broken heart.

God Is Sovereign

God knows all things past, present, and future. He has authority over all things seen and unseen in both the earthly and heavenly realms. God sees beyond our present circumstances; he knows the future and always has a plan regardless of our choices or what is happening around us. In Isaiah 55:8–9, God said: "For my thoughts are not your thoughts, neither are your ways my ways, declares the LORD. For as the heavens are higher than the earth, so are my ways higher than your ways and my thoughts than your thoughts" (ESV). We cannot always understand God's sovereignty, but our faith in him gives us the assurance he is working for our good and on our behalf even when life serves us a bitter cup.

KNOWING GOD

There is so much to hold on to here. Even when all is gone—friends and family, vocation or ministry, your life's work, a home, your means, your reputation, even hope for a future—there is still one thing you can hang on to. It's the one thing that got Christ through his horrific crucifixion. He had everything stripped from him, ripped from his grasp. He went through a mock trial and unthinkable brutality, leading him to the cross. He hung those hours in agony surrounded by a taunting crowd then endured the dark of the grave. But one thing raised him to a new, invincible morning. One thing helped him leave the old things behind. One thing enabled him to step into a garden of new possibilities. That one thing was the intimate relationship he had with his Father. Knowing his Father gave him the hope and strength he needed to drink the cup he was served the day he hung on that cross. You, too, can have the same intimate relationship—a relationship that can offer healing, hope, and freedom amid your suffering.

SEEING FROM GOD'S POINT OF VIEW

So here is where you begin. Knowing what you believe about God helps you understand he is for you and not against you. You are able to see your circumstance from a different perspective. The question of why becomes a little easier to surrender. When you let go of why, you ask a different question. Asking another question will give you a larger view beyond the moment of why and beyond all the hurt and *how come?* Rather than circling the question of *why God allowed your tragedy to happen*, ask yourself *what you believe about God*. Christ knew the truth about his Father, and this gave him strength and courage to see things differently and to trust his Father. By knowing the truth about who God is, you too can possess the same strength and courage to broaden your vision to see as God sees. Just like God gave Jesus supernatural strength and courage, he will also give you the same amount of strength and courage to move through your circumstance.

Making this change in your thinking is hard because we see things in human time and terms. It's so tempting to conclude, *If things are good, so is God, and if things are bad, well, then God must be bad as well.* But the nature of God does not depend upon our circumstances. He doesn't change when our circumstances change.

Whatever you're stuck on thinking God has done or not done, allowed or not allowed, can be keeping you in a painful place. Looking more closely at the nature of God to gain the depth and understanding of who he is and what he has promised will take you in a completely different direction. Your belief about God, yourself, and your circumstances begin to change, bringing you peace and comfort as well as direction and purpose. His Word promises us hope for our future. "'For I know the plans I have for you,' says the LORD. 'They are plans for good and not for disaster, to give you a future and a hope'" (Jeremiah 29:11 NLT).

Having the hope to see a brighter future, a place of peace and love ahead, can lift you from the dark places. It's as if you are sinking in stormy waters, and you see a life raft being tossed your way, or a rescue ship coming for you, or a lighthouse beaming from the dry ground on a nearby shore. It gives you everything you need to both hang on to and to reach out.

Once you know what you believe about God and his promises to you, then you can see with his vision, which is way beyond our own. Viewing things as God views them is key because God sees without the limitations of time or space. He knows the end result.

I thought about this recently when talking with my son about photography. We both love to take pictures but approach doing so in totally different ways. When I take photos, I'm most interested in zeroing in on a person. The background is always secondary. In fact, it drives me crazy to take a picture when there isn't anyone I know in it. When I scan through the photos I've taken, I love to see the faces of people I know and love.

My son isn't fixed on making sure there are people in his photos, regardless of those people being total strangers or loved ones. Instead, he'll spend a tedious amount of time using a wide-angle lens to capture the beauty of the scenery before him, the whole of a landscape without one person in the picture.

When we went on trips and photographed things together, this drove me nuts. I'd watch and wait on Christopher to get the perfect image. Then I'd nudge him to put a person in the picture to make it more interesting and help the scene come alive.

He wouldn't budge. He said placing someone in the scene ruined what he was trying to do, which was to capture the beauty of the natural landscape without distractions. Too often, he argued, photographers focus so much on getting a person posed just so in a beautiful place that they miss capturing the beauty already there.

This baffled me until I flipped through some of his photographs. I was stunned. The panoramic views were astonishing. Beautiful. He was right. The big picture was so much more interesting and alive than I ever imagined. I had focused on a face or two, when there was a much bigger world, so much more to see. It was amazing.

This is how it is when you are hurting. You only see what is right in front of you—your loss, hardship, heartbreak, sorrow—and rightfully so. But this limited view isolates your surroundings and puts a spotlight on all of your pain. This narrow vision hinders you from seeing or feeling anything else. You focus on what has been taken away or unjustly given to another person or wrongfully, hurtfully done to you. There can be so much more to the story, but all you know is how much you hurt and how unfair the circumstances seem.

Looking beyond what is right in front of you may be impossible in times of despair because it is true that your own strength may not fortify you enough to expand your vision to see anything beyond your pain. This is why people look for an escape, whether it is a substance or a distraction. It is an attempt to run away from the despairing sorrow, even if it is only for a brief moment. Running away or getting stuck in your pain is not what God wants for you. He does not want you to be swallowed up in despair or numb from some kind of substance.

There are so many times when individuals become consumed with grief, and they feel as though they are posing for a picture in front of the Grand Canyon, one of the great wonders of the world, and saying, "Hey, do you see me? I am over here. Look at me."

BELIEVING IS SEEING

That is what most people want, after all—for God to see them, to know them; to be understood, heard, and granted favor by him—but they are too busy trying to get God's attention. They miss seeing the expanded scene that surrounds them. All they see is the pain. The way out of their sorrow is for them to look past their circumstances to see what God sees: there are edges to the Grand Canyon. There is a beginning. There is an end.

Knowing there will be an end to something terrible brings huge relief—because when you're in a bad place, you feel as though you're going to be stuck there forever. The loneliness, hurt, frustration, anger, and loss seem unending. You shut down because you can't bear any more agony. Shutting down is what Lisa did. Why put herself out there with friends, family, work, a social life if there would be more agony? She already had more than she could bear.

It's easy to get to that place of not seeing a bigger picture, the Grand Canyon that God sees, because terrible things can be so blinding.

When my daughter was in grade school, she fell and broke her collarbone. She had broken this bone before; the first time was a hairline fracture that over-the-counter pain relievers and a sling for four weeks helped remedy. This time, though, her collarbone broke cleanly and completely in two. Advil wasn't going to help. She was in incredible pain.

The doctor ordered her to wear a sling again and hold her arm and shoulder just so, and he directed her not to move for a couple of weeks. She couldn't have if she wanted to—the pain was too great.

She remained in that sling, relatively motionless, for two months. She cried every time she tried to sit up or walk during the first week. I wanted to cry too. Watching my daughter experience such pain and not being able to take it away or do anything was painful for me as well. I sat next to her and tried to comfort her with my words and gentle touches.

"The pain will lessen a little each day," I reassured her. "Let's just get through today."

But Maddie couldn't think about anything other than how badly she felt at that moment. Finally, at wit's end, she tearfully pleaded for me to pray for her.

I marveled at the natural wisdom of a child—my child. I gently placed my hands on her and began asking God to help her focus on something other than the pain. Whenever I prayed for her, she would finally drift off to sleep. She looked peaceful in her slumber, and the rest was a great relief for both of us. Still, hurt lingered for Maddie and for me. I knew the moment she would wake up, the reality of her pain would be back, and she would feel hurt all over again in full force.

So, again, I would pray.

This went on for more than a week, praying away the pain so Maddie could drift asleep, praying for new strength as she slept so she could endure one more day—and the most interesting thing happened. Every day, the pain lessened a little bit more. Every day, she healed just a little more.

Through it all, I realized what a picture this was of emotional hurt, pain, and healing. When you're emotionally hurt, grieving a loss, reeling in sadness, adrift in frustration or anger, all other matters fade away. Your thoughts can be so powerful that you can't seem to overcome them. You think you can't bear it. You feel like the pain will never end. You can't think about or see anything else. It's like photographing the landscape. When you're focused on the faces, you never fully see all that's around you.

But God sees. He not only sees what you're enduring—he sees the other side of it. He's there. There's power in calling on him to help you get through, to touch you with reassurance, hold you with love, strengthen you in ways you may not see or feel or be aware of, just as Maddie was strengthened and healed even as she slept.

The last thing Maddie wanted to do when she was in so much pain was get up, but doing so facilitated her healing. As uncomfortable and painful as this was, it was necessary for her healing. It took many times of trying and working at getting up and enduring that pain before she could walk. And every time she tried, I was there with reassurance, and God was there too. Our presence didn't magically take away the pain, but it gave her just enough courage and strength to sit and then stand and then to take a step and another until she was walking again.

God will help you move forward when you're tempted to give up and shut down. You tell yourself it hurts too much, so you remain paralyzed, but not moving forward will keep you from healing.

God sees and understands your pain, but he also sees your whole life beyond this terrible moment. When you are willing to see as he sees—to look beyond the pain—he can release you from all the hurt into a bigger picture, a grand place. He will sit with you, walk alongside you, pick you up, and go forward with you. He sees a bigger picture, has a bigger plan, and can invite you into a different world of possibility.

Keep your eyes on God. Keep looking to him to help you see the bigger picture of your life beyond this painful moment and circumstance.

THE LIFE BEYOND

When I was younger, my pastor would end every service with the phrase "God is good all the time."

Over the years, I've repeated this platitude. The thing is, I love God and trust him. I believe him when he says he is good, that he loves me and will never forsake me.

But when Lisa's world fell apart, could I really say that? Isn't it too easy to say "God is good" when goodness surrounds you? What about when goodness doesn't seem evident at all?

Recently, my pastor told a story about a young man who put this question to the test.

Since birth, this man had suffered a rare genetic disease that made his muscles calcify as he grew. The older he became, the more his body stiffened. He became trapped inside, immobilized. Physicians from all around the world came to visit. They wanted to help, and, more, they wanted to learn about this rare disease. They poked and prodded and asked all sorts of questions. The young man became the talk of their medical community. He received other attention too, including visits from celebrities like the Dallas Cowboys cheerleaders, to encourage him. Churches across the country began to pray for him. Our church congregation prayed continually for his healing and deliverance. He prayed as well—fervently.

"It made sense for God to heal him," our pastor said one day. "Think how his miraculous healing would demonstrate God's power to the entire medical community and world."

But healing never came. Nothing helped. Not the medical attention, not the prayer. The young man's condition never improved. Still, despite the pain and immobility, he never stopped hoping for release from the disease. He never stopped believing in the goodness of God. He solicited help to get to church every Sunday to worship and praise God. Every Monday, he sent our pastor an email sharing how much the church's prayers and Sunday's message meant to him and how he would apply the principles from the sermon in the coming week.

This routine carried on for several years, all while the man's health worsened. Finally, he was immobile in his body and unable to be transported to church. Once a week, our pastor visited the man in his home.

On one visit, after a long talk, the two men sat in silence. There seemed to be nothing left to say. It was clear, this man's life was ending. Finally, our pastor wondered aloud, "Have you ever questioned God about why—why me, why this disease, why no healing?"

The young man laughed. "If I had been healed, I never would have met the Dallas Cowboy cheerleaders." They both laughed until drifting into another long silence.

The dying man finally asked, "Do you even know how many medical doctors and researchers I've met?"

Our pastor shook his head. "No."

"I've had the privilege of sharing my testimony and love for Christ with so many, I've lost count. If I hadn't been ill, I would never have encountered such opportunities with so many people dedicated to healing others who didn't know or believe in Christ." He paused. "Maybe . . . ," he ventured, "maybe I was the one who made a difference in them finding salvation."

Our pastor left the young man's house that day for what he knew would be the last time. Overcome, he poured his emotion onto paper:

> When does the thorn become a blessing?
> When does the pain become a friend?
> When does the weakness make me stronger?
> When does my faith make me whole again?
> I want to feel His arms around me

> In the middle of my raging storm
>
> So that I can see the blessing in the thorn
>
> I've heard it said the strength of Christ
>
> Is perfect in my weakness
>
> And the more that I go through
>
> The more I prove the promise true
>
> His love will go to any length
>
> And reaches even now to where I am
>
> But tell me once again, Lord,
>
> I have to ask You
>
> On the cross, You suffered through
>
> Was there a time You ever doubted?
>
> What You already knew?

The words our pastor wrote that day became a song he would introduce to us. His friend's life was the inspiration. That inspiration became an anthem millions of others would sing in the face of struggle and grief: "The Blessing in the Thorn."

In his last days, our pastor's young friend didn't let himself focus on why he did not get healed. Rather he turned his attention to what he believed to be true about God; he realized his purpose was not in his healing, but in being a witness to what he'd experienced—and to the people who surrounded him, the doctors and caregivers, ministers and attendants. He shared his story and his hope. He told people his eyes were fixed on Jesus, and who knows the ripple effect of all he shared. He shared with doctors who had come from around the world to study his disease. He shared with a cheerleading squad that traveled the country and appeared on television to millions of viewers. He shared with his pastor, who sang the praise of his hope to not just our church but people who would carry that song all across the globe for generations. This young man took his eyes off his circumstances and found himself in the same place Jesus found himself that night in Gethsemane.

Please, Jesus begged his Father, *please, let this cup pass from me.*

Jesus had endured so much and done everything his Father had asked him to do. Friends had gathered around him and even followed him to Gethsemane. But in this place, he was alone. The world was sleeping, and Jesus was in agony with only a prayer.

And yet, even prayer was not going to save him from his destiny—the bigger picture. Jesus was called to walk down this impossible path, to endure unbearable suffering and face the ultimate agony when his Father turned his face away. How was Christ able to accept this bitter cup and completely surrender his will?

He unequivocally knew his Father loved him. Jesus had trusted God's bigger plan. Because Jesus had the courage to drink the cup, we now have the gift of salvation. His sacrifice for our sin allows us to know God in the same way Christ knew him. Jesus was able to trust his Father and be confident he could see past the cross. God saw the end result—our salvation. Because Christ trusted his Father, he was able to say, "Nevertheless, not my will, but yours, be done" (Luke 22:42 ESV). With that, he rose, awakened the others, and began the long walk to the cross.

When does the thorn become the blessing?

I think about that line from my pastor's song, that young man's life, Jesus' long walk to save us. Yes: *The Lord's love will go to any length . . . but tell me once again.*

When you enter God's presence, this is exactly what he will do: reassure you of his love, his faithfulness, his comfort, and his healing. He will give you his peace and remind you of his plan to give you hope and a future. He will remind you that he made you on purpose and for a purpose. And you will no longer be fixed on "why?" You will be able to ask a new question: "What do I believe?" and "What do I do next?" These questions will steady your boat and keep you anchored in God's truth and promises.

HELPFUL TOOLS

1. If your why is unanswerable, pray and ask God to help you let it go.
2. Write down the things that will keep you anchored during this storm.
3. Write down the things that will untether you from the things that keep you anchored.
4. Ask yourself what you believe about your circumstances.
5. Write down the biblical truths you can hold on to so as to steady your boat in the midst of your storm.
6. Ask yourself what you believe to be true about God.
7. Write down his attributes and read over them each day in your quiet time.
8. Expand your vision to see things as God sees them. Focus on moving your vision away from what is right in front of you and recognize the beauty that surrounds you beyond your pain.
9. Surrender your hurt, fear, and suffering to God. Ask God to show you a path to finding purpose in your pain.
10. Set aside a time each day to read the Word of God, listen to worship and praise music, meditate and pray. Get to know God personally and intimately.

2
A Cup of Doubt
How to Trust in God's Deliverance Either Through or Out of Your Circumstance

*P*eople streamed through the front door as I set out more snacks, hors d'oeuvres, and desserts on the table. I rearranged the centerpiece of flowers one last time, awaiting the arrival of my friends and family. When the doorbell rang, and my friends made their way inside, every new face I saw generated a huge smile I could not hide—my face glowed with pride. Being surrounded by the familiarity and comfort of my friends filled me. Our little boy, who was now eight years old and already in the second grade, was going to be baptized today in our swimming pool. Where had the time gone? It seemed like only yesterday he was learning to walk. Now, on this beautiful sunny afternoon, he decided to declare publicly his decision to live for Christ. Christopher's admission of his faith filled my heart with joy. We had carefully planned a celebration for our family, dearest friends, and church family to witness this beautiful moment. Our pastor would perform the baptism, and my mom and dad were on their way, making the three-hour drive from Dallas. My husband stood on the back patio tending to the hamburgers on the grill and watching the guests stir. Sunlight washed over him and reflected in magical beams off the pool where the baptism would take place.

Such a beautiful day, I thought, keeping an eye on the door for my parents. I felt content in every way for my friends and family, my home, and this celebration; mostly, for my son's heart and God's goodness to each of us. *Sunshine*, I thought. *Redemption. Perfect.*

Isn't this what happens in the middle of blessings? We get caught up in a moment, and we're deceived into thinking life is perfect. Our expectations rise—but disappointment lurks in the shadows. We push them aside as best we can, but without warning, the unthinkable happens—tragedy strikes.

Mom and Dad appeared at the door, and we hugged quickly. I then turned my attention to our pastor announcing for everyone to gather for a prayer of blessing over the food we were about to eat. *This is like communion*, I thought as people piled their plates with our little feast and sat all around the house and in the backyard to fellowship and celebrate with us. Our friends chatted, joked, and laughed. As monumental a day as this was for our son's baptism, I realized that sitting in stillness, taking in the beauty of the moment, and laughing with friends is what made the day complete. I caught my husband's eye at one point, and the mutual pride we each felt for Christopher was so real, like one of those sunbeams.

Afternoon slid into evening, and I glanced around to find Mom and Dad to share the love with them too. For the first time that day, I realized that we hadn't really talked, and I missed them. *Where were they?* I scanned all the faces in the backyard. Normally they would be in the center of all the activity, or at least near me. When I finally spotted them, they were at the fringe of the yard, backed far away from the clusters of people. They seemed so distant, and not just because of where they stood. I caught Mom's eye, and she smiled back, but not with the shared joy I had expected—more as if on autopilot, more melancholy, forced.

The sun was beginning to set, and people were drifting to the door, calling it an evening. When the guests were finally gone and the kids were winding down with a movie in the family room, Mom whispered to me, "Connie, we have to talk." The seriousness in her tone startled me. The kitchen, a center of laughter just minutes ago, seemed suddenly somber.

Why was she whispering?

"Mom, what's wrong?"

Her eyes watered. "Connie, three days ago, your dad was indicted by the federal government on seven counts of mail fraud. He's facing ten years in prison." *Dad indicted? By the US government? For mail fraud?* None of this was adding up. I wanted to laugh. Surely this was a joke. But Mom and Dad were no longer even trying to force smiles. I studied their faces and noticed the dark circles under their eyes. The day I thought had been perfect and golden, like those beautiful sunbeams, suddenly turned dark.

LOSING HOPE

I have always looked up to and greatly admired my father. He taught me everything I knew about being faithful and living for God. He and my mother brought me up to go to church every Sunday. We never missed. If we were sick, we went to church to be healed; if we were on vacation, we stopped and went to church. My dad was a man of his word. If he said he was going to do something, then you knew with certainty he was going to do it. I loved my dad, and like most daughters, I adored his attention and approval.

My dad had retired from his management position from a large company several years earlier to run his own company building assisted living homes for the elderly. He seemed happy and in his element. Life was good.

After that fateful evening of my son's baptism, I learned the whole story. My dad's company had used government money to build some of the assisted living centers. The money from the government was supposed to be used to pay the contractors within seven days of their labor. Instead, my dad's chief financial officer had taken that money and used it to pay other bills, and the contractors never got paid. Though my father never knew this was happening, he was responsible because he owned the company. However, my dad admitted to being responsible but only guilty on one of the seven counts of fraud. He had made a gentleman's agreement with a fellow contractor to pay him later in the month. The two of them were good friends and often bartered services. This decision was a misstep that would cost my dad his freedom. Because of this, he knew he could not defend his innocence against the government, so he and his lawyer were negotiating a plea deal.

As I sat there listening to my parents explain, fear began to overtake all my senses. I could not believe what they were telling me. I felt my heart begin to race and sweat drip down my forehead. I wanted to run away as far as I could to escape the foreboding reality that my dad could go to prison.

Later that night, I could not sleep. Desperate for comfort and peace, I rolled out of bed and slowly made my way to my closet, where I changed into my swimsuit. I gently padded down the dimly lit stairs through the kitchen and into the empty and silent backyard. Under the canopy of the dark sky, I crawled into the warmth of our hot tub and cried for what seemed like hours. *This is too much.*

THE DECISION

After meeting with our attorney, we all agreed Dad's best option was to accept a plea bargain. This agreement would guarantee a shorter prison sentence of three to five years and would take the possibility of a seven-to ten-year sentence off the table. When an individual is sentenced to prison in federal court, there is no parole; they are given the time they serve. Our lawyer told me I had to address the judge in court and speak on Dad's behalf. As it turned out, a judge was assigned to his case who had a reputation of being harsh. Our hopes of my dad receiving little to no prison time were dim.

On his day in court, we made our way into the ominous courtroom where we all knew his fate would be decided within the hour. Our family and friends filled every seat inside the room where his sentencing would occur.

I felt ill. By the look on the judge's face, he had already made his decision before the proceedings even began. Mercy was not on my dad's side. I had a sinking feeling.

The pressure of speaking to the judge on behalf of my dad's character began to overwhelm me. Fear washed over me like a massive wave, and I started shaking. A dear friend took me into the hallway and prayed over me to calm my nerves. I felt God's peace. With the help of God's strength and his comforting presence surrounding me, I boldly stood before the judge and told him what a hardworking, loving, and good man my father was.

As I began to share my story, the judge's empty eyes stared at me coldly and flat. Undaunted, I continued to affectionately describe my dad's true nature and character. Halfway through my testimony, something unexpected happened. The judge's face changed, and his eyes softened. I knew without a doubt it was the Holy Spirit working in the heart and mind of the judge. Something miraculous was happening.

Could it be that my dad would not have to serve time in federal prison? We knew he did not deserve to be there, but could this judge, who had the reputation of being the toughest in his district, actually see it that way?

As the judge began to declare his ruling, he said these words with a perplexed look on his face: "I cannot believe I am doing this, but I am going to cut his sentence in half." Cutting his sentence in half was a motion called a downward departure. The judge made this decision based on Dad's character and all the efforts he had initiated to right the wrongs done by his company. Through God's power, the judge had experienced a change of heart. This decision, we later discovered, was unheard of in his court. This judge had never issued a downward departure before, and he was over seventy years old! While he didn't allow my dad to walk away without prison time, a miracle had happened nonetheless.

Our emotions were raw. On the one hand, we were grateful that my dad's sentence had been cut in half; but on the other hand, my dad was on his way to prison. Even though we knew God had demonstrated his power in the courtroom, we were still overcome with uncertainty.

FACING REALITY

I felt an unbearable pain and devastation in the days and weeks after I had learned of my dad's indictment. First, I was in shock, numb to the reality of the pain that lay ahead, and then disbelief. When the truth finally sunk its razor-sharp teeth deep into my heart, my emotions began to unravel at a speed I could not stop. My dad was my rock, my spiritual giant, the man I looked to for guidance and advice. Now a shadow of shame had been cast on him, and the reality of prison loomed over me like a recurring nightmare, haunting me night after night. *What will happen to him?* Fear gripped me. *What will his days look like? His nights? This shouldn't have happened. This isn't fair. I'm so scared.* I was spinning.

DO THE NEXT THING

The following day, I got out of bed feeling like this had all been a bad dream. I was numb. Then I suddenly realized it wasn't a bad dream at all—it was real.

The emotions came rushing in—fear, anger, depression—then nausea hit me like a wave. This was when I knew I had to limit my thoughts and *just do the next thing*. I made myself a cup of hot tea, grabbed my favorite blanket, and headed to the small corner room where I could be alone with God.

Some days all I could do was listen to praise music. Praise and worship replaced my heartache with enough peace to get me to do the next thing. Take a shower, get dressed, wake the kids, make breakfast—*do the next thing*. When the emotions rushed back in like a tidal wave, I went to my little room. If I was driving when the flood began, I would pull over to the side of the road and put in my earphones with soft music playing in the background. I would pray until I felt enough peace to get me to *do the next thing*.

When you are drinking a cup of doubt, limiting your thoughts and simply doing the next thing helps you get through the day. When emotions paralyze you, look up, reach out, and *do the next thing*. This exercise will help maintain hope and will encourage you to keep moving ahead and looking forward.

HOW DID WE GET HERE?

When my dad was in prison, the only thing that got him through the long, scary days was knowing who God was. God was not only his anchor but ours as well. We had similar days outside the prison. We were scared for him, lonely for him, and sad for him. God filled our days with courage, peace, and hope.

The first day I walked into that federal prison, I thought to myself, *Why am I here? I do not belong here—we do not belong here. This is a place for bad people, criminals, liars, and cheats. Not my dad! He is a Christian, a deacon in the church, a dad, a granddad.* The waiting room had concrete floors and concrete benches. Dingy gray walls and dim lighting made the mood even worse. As I surveyed the people in the room, I felt out of place, overdressed, like I was painted glaring red in a black and white movie. In my mind, it seemed everyone was staring at me, and God felt a million miles away.

I had been instructed to bring my personal belongings in a see-through bag. I stood there with all the items I had packed into my new clear bag on display for everyone to see. Feeling humiliated, I waited for my name to be called to see my dad for the first time behind locked doors. When the stoic armed guard called my name, I nervously walked to the stand where he dumped the contents of my bag onto the counter while I watched him carefully inspect each item for contraband.

When the guard cleared me to go into the prison to see my dad, another emotionless armed guard dressed in a starched black and white uniform escorted me into a small holding room behind a thick barred door that slid open and clanked shut behind me. In front of me was another large, locked door waiting to be opened by the same foreboding guard. I stood in this holding area for what seemed an eternity, waiting for the prison doors to open on the other side. In what felt like slow motion, the guard grabbed a key from his overcrowded key ring and placed it into a lock flush to the wall, turning it counterclockwise. With a jarring knock, the doors slid open. In silence, he led me down a hall as if he was following the rhythm of a marching band whose music I could not hear; only the clump of his steps and the rattling of his keys made a noise. The cadence of each step echoed down the hall and into a room lined only with rows of chairs. He instructed me to take a seat and wait.

The chairs were plastic, the walls were white, and there were two vending machines in the far corner. There was a tall stand where a guard stood watch over the prisoners and guests.

Never in my wildest dreams did I think I would be in this place. The thought screamed in my head: *I do* not *belong here!* I felt betrayed by God. I was angry and doubted his love for me in that moment. My dad had served God all his life. We never missed church. He led Bible studies, taught Sunday school, and volunteered whenever possible. We begged God to spare my dad from going to prison. We fasted. We prayed. My faith could not have been stronger. But here we were!

The longer I sat there in that hard plastic chair, the angrier I became. I wanted to get up right then and leave, but I couldn't—I was locked in. Then I looked up and saw my dad coming toward me: the man I admired, who I thought could do no wrong, the man who taught me as a little girl to love Jesus. He now stood before me wearing black thick-soled shoes, khaki pants, and a long-sleeved shirt with black numbers stamped over the front pocket. He looked straight at me, appearing calm and rested as if he had seen God himself.

At first, I did not understand. I had expected my dad to be distraught, overwhelmed with sadness, fear, anger—I thought he'd have all the emotions I was having, but he had none of these. He started weeping as he shared what God was telling him during this time of solitude. My dad had already spent two weeks there, and as "luck" would have it, he initially ended up in a room by himself. We know this was not luck. It was the hand of God keeping him safe and putting him in a place where God knew there would be limited distractions. God had a captivated audience with my dad in this place of solitude. God began speaking love into his heart.

In all of his years of knowing about Jesus, my dad explained he did not have a close personal relationship with him and never felt his unconditional love. But his first two weeks of prison had changed his relationship with Christ. He described feeling an overwhelming sense of love that gave him hope, peace, and comfort—feelings he had not experienced prior to being in prison. As he calmly shared his heart, I took in a deep breath and exhaled. The feelings of betrayal and anger began to slide off of me. I had never seen my dad so tender. He took my hands, and we prayed right there in front of everyone. We did not care who saw us. In that quiet moment of prayer, God reminded me to trust and look to him because he would carry me through. A little bit of hope began to fill my cup.

OUR NEW REALITY

Each day I walked down the path of uncertainty, God showed me pieces of his truth. But one morning, his peace eluded me when my mom asked me to pray for Dad because something had happened, and he was having a bad day. That was all she said—all I knew was *he was having a bad day.*

I reacted in fear and thought the worst. I wanted to give in to my feelings and stay in bed, but I had small children to tend to, so that was not an option. I dragged around the house for a few hours, thinking of all the bad things that could have happened. I prayed, but the prayers felt hollow. I kept thinking, *What if someone hurt him?* The thought was so intrusive I could not shake it.

I kept on doing what I needed to do throughout the morning. After lunch, I was rocking my baby to sleep for a nap, listening to worship music playing softly in the background, when I heard the words "Be still and know I am God." The song went on to say, "Hide me now under your wings and cover me within your mighty hands." I began to weep. I felt God's presence right there in my daughter's nursery as I held her in my arms. Through that song, I heard God whisper, *I will protect your dad, and I will carry you through this storm—trust in me.* I felt his warmth wash over me. It was a difficult week, but I stayed the course by keeping my eyes on Christ and trusting him.

That day in the rocking chair, I decided to let go and allow God to carry me through this painful journey. I trusted God would take my dad and me above the storm. He would protect us both in different ways. God's plan was to deliver us *through* this circumstance instead of immediately *out* of it. I could not drink this cup without God's supernatural strength. My trust in him would waver, but it never collapsed.

BEING DELIVERED THROUGH

When a crisis makes its ugly way into your life, your first reaction is typically shock and disbelief. When the truth finally settles in, you are left with the cruel aftermath of your unwanted pain. You want the suffering to stop, so you beg God to take the spiraling feelings away. You pray and plead for him to deliver you out of your heartache.

No one likes to endure the anguish of heartbreak. It's too painful. You tell yourself it would be much better if God would simply give you relief from your unwanted grief. Is that too much to ask? Does God really require everyone to walk through their pain, to push beyond their comfort zone, and to persevere past their adversity to change?

Walking through tragedy can reshape who you are, but God does not require a crisis for you to make a change. Bad things happen to good people. And when bad things occur, you can either move forward or stand still. Both are difficult and agonizing, especially when you feel as though God has let you down. But moving forward, knowing God is with you and is for you, progresses you toward healing. Standing still keeps you stuck in your grief. Believing God is responsible for your circumstance leaves you feeling dismissed, abandoned, and betrayed by him. These feelings are why it is often difficult to move past doubt and into faith. You are tempted to doubt God and believe he does not love you and doesn't care enough to remove your pain and suffering.

In counseling, my clients, who were weary from the relentless pain they were enduring day after day, would ask me when their suffering would end. They doubted God's love and faithfulness and questioned his ability to help them. They asserted God felt absent and far away. They wanted to know why God had not healed them of their heartache or delivered them from their sorrow.

I would explain God had not abandoned them, and he had heard their cries, but there are occasions when God will deliver you *through* your circumstances, and there are times when he will deliver you *out* of them. But even when you find yourself walking through your heartache, God is still delivering you.

Think about that for a minute and let this truth sink in. You live in a world where you can get most of what you want at a moment's notice. You can order something online and receive it that same day. You drive through fast-food restaurants to get your food within minutes. You surf the internet, and within seconds you have your answer. You don't have to wait a week to watch another episode of your favorite show because you can binge-watch the whole season at one time. You live in a society of immediate results. Why wouldn't you want God to heal you from your pain immediately?

You may find yourself feeling offended, upset, or agitated by the idea that God may choose to deliver you through your pain rather than out of it. You may think to yourself, *Through!? That is not okay, it is too long; I don't want to go through this circumstance; I want to be delivered out now!* These were the exact thoughts I had when first learning about my dad's possible prison sentence.

I remember the day of Christopher's baptism as if it were yesterday. When I learned my dad might go to prison for ten years, I thought, *God, you have to deliver us out of this. Please do not make my dad walk through a prison sentence.* I dug my heels in and demanded God to deliver all of us out of the nightmare, to spare my dad, my mom, and myself from the heartache of prison. In the end, God chose not to deliver my dad or my family directly out of that circumstance, but he did deliver us through it.

Because the pain and sorrow are so intense, you naturally want God to remove them from your life immediately. When you don't acknowledge and believe God is able and willing to walk you through your suffering, especially when it takes longer than you want, you often become more irritable and discontented. You run the risk of falling deeper into your pain and anguish. In desperation for relief, you find yourself repeatedly asking, even demanding, God to instantly deliver you out of your tragedy. In your suffering, though, you fail to understand God does have a plan, but it may be different from what you expected. Letting go of doubt and trusting in God's faithfulness, mercy, and love to deliver you through your pain will give you the strength and courage to keep moving forward.

I have seen God deliver individuals directly out of their suffering, but more often, I see him delivering people through them. *Why?* Here we are back at this nagging question. Why do we have to walk through painful experiences? Sometimes there is no easy answer.

When you discover there is no easy answer for *why*, it is time to pull back and expand your vision to see things from God's perspective. As we discussed in chapter 1, stepping back to see things as God sees them will enable you to change your point of view. Walking through your circumstances will allow you to come out on the other side changed. As with my dad, your circumstance can redefine your relationship with Christ and refine your character. Like metal that goes through fire, once you are heated, you come out purified.

In the Bible, as well, we can find instances where God delivered people directly out of their tragedy and other times when he delivered them through it. For example, God immediately delivered the Israelites out of the hands of the Egyptians through the parting of the Red Sea, but he delivered Joseph through abuse, slavery, and prison. Both were delivered from their circumstances. For the Israelites, it was immediate, but for Joseph, it was not; his deliverance took years.

THE PRISONER

Joseph was a man whose circumstances were completely unfair and totally out of his control. He was taken from his home, tossed into a pit, sold into slavery, falsely accused, and then thrown into prison. Joseph lost everything, including his dignity. It would appear God had completely abandoned him.

Joseph was the son of Jacob, a God-fearing man who was the father of what would eventually be the twelve tribes of Israel. Jacob and his wife Rachel were advanced in their years when Joseph was born. Jacob had many other sons from his first wife, Leah, whom he was tricked into marrying. His true love was Rachel, but she could not bear him a child. So, when Rachel announced she was going to have a baby, I imagine Jacob was thrilled, and when she gave birth to a son, he wasn't just thrilled; he was over-the-moon happy. The woman whom he cherished and loved dearly had finally given him a son, a miracle baby.

Joseph was his father's favorite. Jacob boasted about his son Joseph and never tried to hide how much he loved him more than his brothers. I imagine Jacob spent hours teaching Joseph how to become a man who loved and followed the ways of God. Without a doubt, this favoritism he so brazenly showed Joseph planted seeds of jealousy into the hearts of Joseph's older brothers.

Jacob stitched together a beautifully embellished robe when Joseph was a young boy, which symbolized Jacob's adoration for his son. It was a seemingly wonderful gift from his father at the time, but this lavish gesture backfired as it triggered a path of hardship for Joseph. When Joseph's brothers discovered their father had given him a special hand-woven robe, jealousy burrowed deeper into their already envious and resentful hearts.

To make matters worse, Joseph had a dream he foolishly felt compelled to share with his jealous brothers. He told them they were all in a field bundling grain when suddenly his bundle of grain stood straight up and theirs bowed down to his. As if that wasn't bad enough, he later told them of another dream in which the sun, moon, and eleven stars, which represented his parents and eleven brothers, also bowed down to him. His brothers were furious. They mocked the very idea they would someday bow down to their overindulged little brother. These dreams only added fuel to his brothers' already simmering, contentious, and angry fire of jealousy. Sharing those dreams without considering the consequence set the course for the rest of Joseph's life.

One day when all of Joseph's brothers were in the fields tending their father's flock, they devised a plan to kill their spoiled little brother. However, when one of the brothers, Reuben, heard of this plan, he stopped them. Rather than killing Joseph, they stripped him of his cherished robe and threw him into a deserted well. When the brothers saw an Ishmaelite caravan making its way into Egypt, they pulled Joseph out of the pit and decided to sell him for a few pieces of silver. Having been abused by his brothers and now alone, Joseph was at the mercy of his new slave owners. Within moments Joseph went from favored son to humbled slave. Where was God? I am sure Joseph cried out for help. "Almighty God, please deliver me out of the hands of these vicious people!" But it did not appear God heard his cries.

This turn in fate set a series of tragic circumstances in motion. It seemed as though God had turned his back on Joseph. Being accused of something he did not do, Joseph ended up in prison for many years. A young boy so favored by his father had a life full of potential ahead of him, but he spent the prime of his life behind lock and key because of that fateful day with his brothers. Why would God allow such a thing? Where was God in the midst of his trauma?

Reading stories in the Bible like Joseph's can give you insight into your own circumstances. Joseph's story can offer you hope and courage to walk through your own struggles. Let's drill deeper into his story and learn from his rearview mirror the purpose of being delivered through a circumstance rather than out of it.

Considering God's all-powerful nature, it would seem to make sense for God to reach down from heaven and immediately rescue Joseph from his current misery. But this was not what happened. God had other plans.

Though God did not instantly deliver Joseph out of slavery, he did grant him favor and give him his protection. Amazingly, Joseph did not turn his back on God or abandon his faith. Instead, he believed God had a plan for him and would undoubtedly see him through.

FOLLOWING THE PATH

When you feel like your faith is failing you, you have to be like Joseph and continue walking the path in front of you even though the road seems dark. So often, in the middle of hardship and pain, all you can see is your hurt and suffering—your feelings and circumstances that are staring right at you. In the case of Joseph, all he could see was the assault his brothers so brutally launched upon him, resulting in the loss of his family and freedom. His life as he knew it was over and would never be the same. So far away from his loving father and his childhood home, he was left alone to nurse his wounds and wonder what tomorrow would bring. Traumatized by his immediate surroundings, he had to lean into his faith in God to trust that things would turn out for his good.

When Joseph arrived in Egypt, a man named Potiphar, the captain of the guard of Pharaoh's army, bought him from the Ishmaelites. You may be thinking, *Wow, what a stroke of luck to be bought by such an important man.* This was not luck; God's hand of favor was placed directly over Joseph for a specific purpose. Even though Joseph was now a slave, God put favor on him so he could begin orchestrating something much bigger in his life. Joseph had no idea what was being coordinated in the supernatural by God. All he could do was continue moving forward toward the path God was forming and trust God was working on his behalf even though he could not see it with his natural eyes.

Joseph settled into his new normal. He worked hard and tried to stay focused on the bigger picture. Potiphar, the slave owner, took notice of Joseph's work ethic and elevated his position to oversee his entire household. God's blessing was on everything Potiphar owned from that moment forward, both in his house and in his field. God had clearly granted Joseph his favor. But it wasn't long before Joseph encountered injustice and tragedy yet again.

Potiphar's wife was attracted to Joseph's physique and good looks, and when Joseph rejected her advances toward him, she accused him of trying to seduce her. Once Potiphar heard the news, he threw Joseph into prison. Though he was innocent, this hardworking and God-fearing man had no one to defend him. Being in prison was now his new fate. Surely this is when Joseph would give up and turn his back on this loving God he was introduced to as a child.

Imagine for a minute being Joseph. Can you see how he might have been overcome with hopelessness, depression, anger, and feelings of betrayal? He was stripped of his clothing, thrown into a pit, abandoned by his brothers, and sold into slavery. Isn't that enough hardship and devastation for any one person? After all the trauma he had endured, a prison sentence just seems cruel. I am not sure I could have taken another step; I would have wanted to give up. How do you have hope when everything seems to go so wrong? Just when you think you see the light at the end of the tunnel, the rug gets ripped out from under you again.

This is what happened to Joseph. He could not get a break. Every time things started looking like they were turning around for him, another terrible thing would happen. Talk about injustice and a reason to be bitter. Joseph had every right to give up on God. Feeling despondent, hopeless, and unable to take another step must be some of what

Joseph felt. He could have easily turned his back on God and walked away. After all, he was spending the prime of his life in prison for a crime he did not commit. He could have been bitter and said to himself, "If it were not for my brothers throwing me in that pit, my life would be so different. I would not be in this kind of pain and suffering." If the prophetic dreams from his youth had come true, Joseph would not be in prison. He would be living a life of privilege and wealth. Joseph's undeserved and unfair circumstances could not have taken a turn farther away from that dream. He was spending his days behind the walls of a darkened prison. In that dark and lonely place, Joseph surrendered his heart.

It is easy for us today to see God's handiwork in Joseph's life, but at the time, it was likely difficult to see how God was going to use this tragedy for good. Joseph had to follow the path he was given and expand his vision to see things from God's point of view. His faith in a loving and sovereign God led him to believe God was working behind the scenes to achieve a greater purpose amid his suffering.

Think about this from Joseph's perspective. He was a slave and a victim of violence at the hand of his own brothers. While being sold into a wealthy family may be the favor of God, he was still a prisoner in a strange household in a foreign land. And what about Joseph's dreams? God had shown him a vision of himself as a man of royal influence. Joseph believed God gave him a promise, but there he sat under the rule of Pharoah, nothing more than a lowly slave. As this reality settled into Joseph's mind, he had to decide which path he was going to take: the path of further emotional destruction or the path of righteousness.

Joseph had to mourn and grieve the loss of his family, home, and dreams. He had to accept that he would most likely never see his father or his home again, and his brothers hated him so much they wanted him dead. Joseph could have easily been consumed with anger and bitterness for having his life and freedom stolen. He could have demanded God deliver him immediately out of this unjust imprisonment. He could have run away and gotten himself into more trouble or taken matters into his own hands. Joseph had every reason to plummet into the depths of hopelessness, to throw in the towel and believe his life was over. After all, he had cried out to God with no immediate results.

Have you ever felt like Joseph? Have you had a situation where you fell into the depth of hopelessness or wanted to throw in the towel? Have you had days when you did not want to live anymore, and out of desperation you cried out to God and felt he did not hear you? Have you ever been tempted to demand deliverance, and when it did not happen, you took matters into your own hands? When life gets tough, running away from all of the pain and hardship or trying everything you can to control them seems appealing. But you learn in this story there is another option.

Joseph was strong in his faith. His father had taught him who God was in his entirety. Joseph knew the sovereignty, the power, the omniscience, and the unconditional love of God, so he held tightly to the faith his father, Jacob, had taught him.

Because of his faith and love for God, Joseph had the ability to move forward. He entrusted him and chose to see and receive God's unmerited favor during his times of hardship and tragedy. As difficult as his circumstances were to endure, Joseph trusted his life was part of a bigger plan. Even though he could not see the end result, deep down, he understood the sovereignty of God and believed God was working out a greater purpose. His hope was in God and God alone. Joseph chose the path of righteous living despite his suffering.

MOVING FORWARD

While in prison, the Lord's favor was with Joseph once again. The prison guard took a special interest in Joseph. He liked him and trusted him. He was so impressed by Joseph's attitude and work ethic that he put him in charge of all the prisoners.

Through a series of unlikely events, Pharoah summoned Joseph to interpret his dreams, and when he did, the Pharaoh was so pleased he released Joseph from prison and put him in charge of the entire land of Egypt. He dressed Joseph in robes of fine linen and put a gold chain around his neck and had him ride in his chariot as the second in command. Wow! Are you thinking what I am thinking? Those dreams were not just the indulging wishful fantasies of a young teenage boy. They were prophetic promises straight from God. Who would have ever thought they would actually come true? Decades later, after Joseph had been thrown into a pit, sold into slavery, falsely accused, and sent to prison, he became second in command in the land of Egypt. Incredible!

You probably won't guess what happened next. Because of a great famine that spread throughout the country, Joseph's brothers had to make the trek from the land of Canaan to Egypt to gather grain that Joseph had wisely stored in warehouses in case of a famine. When his brothers arrived, not recognizing him, they bowed down to him out of reverence to his authority—only to later discover this was their little brother—Joseph, whom they had mocked, abused, and sold.

What a remarkable ending to such a tragic story. God knew all along the end result, but Joseph only had his faith in God and the hope that those prophetic dreams would become a reality one day. His circumstances did not come close to pointing in that direction. Joseph stayed the course, persevered through hardship, tolerated rejection and betrayal, withstood pain, and endured sorrow. He refused to surrender to hopelessness. Joseph radically accepted his circumstances and decisively looked to God for his strength, courage, and hope. Moving forward means you, like Joseph, have to take a drink from the cup you have been served, believing God has a plan to get you through no matter how bitter that cup is.

THE BIGGER PICTURE

Joseph remained loyal, faithful, and true to God throughout his life. He embraced God's peace, serenity, and refinement. By the time Joseph got out of prison, he was a different man. Though the life Joseph had envisioned for himself was stripped from him, he decided to push past his feelings to remain steadfast in his faith and became willing to see the bigger picture God was painting.

It seems unbelievable that Joseph could remain so faithful to God. How did he do it? How could Joseph put his trust in a God who would allow so much wrongdoing in his life and see things from a different perspective? What was it about Joseph that kept him strong? Where was God all those years he was in prison? Through the narrow lens of his circumstances, it would appear that God had deserted him. But when you view his life through God's expanded lens, you see God did not abandon him but was, in fact, with him. He was there comforting, leading, protecting, and refining Joseph.

It is difficult to pull back from your circumstances to see God's expanded view when you are suffering. But looking closely at Joseph's story can give you hope to know God is doing the same in your life as he did in Joseph's. Even though you may be in a dark and lonely place, you, like Joseph, are not alone. God is with you, and he has a greater plan for you—he sees the bigger picture and the end result.

God had Joseph on a path with an end goal in sight, but Joseph could not see the end. He had to trust God was in control and was working to perfect the plan he was forming. This trust required extraordinary faith, perseverance, and a belief that God was moving on his behalf to bring forth purpose in his life despite what was happening around him. The same is true for you. Despite your circumstances and despite what you can't see with your natural eyes, God is working out a purposeful plan in your life. You, like Joseph, have to choose to push past your feelings and trust in God, and be willing to see the bigger picture.

REARVIEW MIRROR

In spite of the remarkable ending in Joseph's story, you might be thinking God wasted all of those years in prison. What good could come out of Joseph sitting in a darkened prison cell?

Your circumstances never limit God. He will use whatever opportunity he can to shape and mold you into who he wants you to become. God used those prison years to refine, teach, and prepare Joseph for what was to come.

When Joseph was young, he was spoiled, presumptuous, and arrogant. But by the time he became ruler, he was a man of great humility, faith, and wisdom. God delivered Joseph, but as you can see from his story, he was delivered through his circumstances instead of instantly out of them. God did not deny Joseph immediate deliverance out of his troubles because Joseph was immature and doubted the existence of God. Quite the opposite. Joseph had extraordinary faith, and his immaturity would not stand in the way of God fulfilling his purpose in

Joseph's life. God did not create the circumstance of Joseph's brothers assaulting him and selling him into slavery; yet, in his sovereignty, he used it to fulfill his plan for Joseph's life.

Year after year, God worked on Joseph's behalf behind the scenes. God knew Joseph needed to have some sharp edges smoothed off before fulfilling those prophetic dreams of him being a ruler, so again he used the unfortunate chain of events to smooth the edges of Joseph's character. Through all of his experiences, God taught Joseph perseverance, submission, and humility. God also provided Joseph with favor in every situation where he needed it. Finally, God opened doors that needed opening and gave Joseph an abundance of courage, grace, and strength to endure all of the treacherous and unfortunate events surrounding him. The end result was God's purpose in Joseph's life being fulfilled. Joseph's life did not happen the way he thought it would, but in the end, those prophetic dreams came true, and God fulfilled his purpose in Joseph's life. Often in your own life, you can see the hand of God more clearly in the rearview mirror. You have the advantage of looking back and seeing how God was working on your behalf. However, while in the middle of your circumstance, you have to lean into your faith to know God is moving even if you cannot see it.

HOW DO WE KEEP FROM DOUBTING GOD?

You may be wondering, *Is the reason people are not delivered out of their situation because they doubt God? Is the reason God has not delivered me because I do not have enough faith?* Doubting God is a stumbling block to your healing, but it is not the reason God chooses to deliver you through your tragedy rather than out of it.

When it seems God is not delivering you from your heartache, doubt makes its way into your heart and mind. Like my clients whose suffering would never seem to end, you may question God's ability to rescue you from your pain.

Doubt can make you feel guilty because Christians are supposed to have faith. They are told faith does not doubt God; faith trusts God. But here you are, reeling in pain and doubting God's willingness to deliver you.

Understanding the principle of God delivering you through your circumstances rather than out of them will help increase your faith. Knowing God is working behind the scenes to deliver you will give you hope. But this hope will diminish if you expect God to immediately deliver you out of your circumstance that is bringing so much pain. Just because you are still hurting and can't see the bigger picture does not mean God is not working. Faith in who God is will keep your eyes focused on him rather than your circumstance.

I am sure Joseph had his doubts. I can imagine he doubted his prophetic dreams would ever become a reality, and there were likely occasions when Joseph doubted God's ability to intervene. He had many opportunities to give up on God, question his ways, and wonder if his truths were real. But Joseph never lost faith. Despite the unjust string of tragedies in his life, Joseph hung on to what he believed to be true about the nature of God.

When you feel as though you are in the dark and God is a million miles away, the tendency is to doubt his ability to work on your behalf based on your feelings or on what you see or do not see within the events occurring in your life. When you rely on your feelings and focus on your circumstances, you will drift farther and farther away from God and deeper and deeper into your pain, like a boat floating in uncharted waters. Changing your perspective and allowing God to comfort you during your suffering will give you hope and wash away your doubt.

MIRACLES OF GOD

Looking for God's miraculous touch throughout your journey will strengthen your faith and show you God's hand of mercy working in the midst of your situation. Let's take another look at Joseph's story and see how this principle plays out in his life.

Joseph was always watching for God's intervention. God first delivered Joseph out of the pit. He then placed him in the care of a master who gave Joseph control of his entire estate. God made sure the prison guard noticed Joseph's character and strong work ethic, causing the guard to elevate his position in prison. God gave Joseph the prophetic gift of interpreting dreams, which eventually led to his favor with Pharoah and his release. Even though God did not immediately deliver Joseph out of his struggles, he was miraculously delivering him through each circumstance, refining, strengthening, and encouraging him along the way.

I saw God's miraculous touch that day in the courtroom when the judge had a change of heart. Even though my dad still had to go to prison, his sentence was cut in half. When Dad was in prison, my mom worried about how she was going to pay her bills. A day or two before a bill was due, something amazing would happen. She would receive an anonymous check in the mail, or someone would ask my mom, a retired hairdresser, to cut their hair, and it would be just enough money to make a necessary payment. The entire time my dad was gone, she was never late paying a bill, and she managed to pay her mortgage on time each month. There were days we had no idea how she was going to do it, but God always provided.

Miracles may not always be extraordinary; they may be subtle, like getting out of bed in the morning, engaging in life, and having the ability to see there is hope. On the days that seem too dark, too depressing, God can miraculously show you his goodness even in the simple things like having the clarity to see the beauty of his creation from your bedroom window. Perhaps it is the spring flowers blooming in the yard, the smile of a child walking to school, or a beautiful sunrise. When you step back and allow God's goodness to envelope you in the handiwork of his creation, you are reminded of his majesty and glory. Not only do you see his hand working, you feel his miraculous touch.

When you pull back and expand your vision to see your life as God sees it, you begin to recognize his supernatural plan starting to unfold. You can feel his presence and witness his promises coming to pass through the small miracles that occur in your life every day.

PATIENCE BREEDS HOPE

Being able to walk through your heartache takes patience. When you stop expecting your grief to immediately end and learn to sit in the tension of sorrow and hope, you will gain perspective. A different outlook will give you the ability to keep moving forward.

When you feel yourself getting overwhelmed or taken under by your heartache, step away and take time to center your thoughts on the promises of God. This will remind you he is with you, and he will give you strength and courage to keep going. In Matthew 11:28 Jesus said, "Come to me, all who labor and are heavy laden, and I will give you rest" (ESV).

Remove any expectations you may have regarding your circumstance. Expectations interfere with your ability to pull back and wait on God. Remind yourself what is important. Each day, tell yourself God is present with you. Even though you may feel abandoned, you are not alone. God's promise to Jacob in Genesis 28 is true for you as well: "I am with you and will keep you wherever you go and will bring you back to this land. For I will not leave you until I have done what I have promised you" (v. 15 ESV). Patience is a gift you give yourself when walking through a difficult circumstance or dealing with a tragic loss. This virtue will allow both you and God time to bring about healing and purpose.

Many times God delivers you in ways you would not have imagined. When your eyes are focused on him, he will see you through. His grace may be sufficient just for the day you ask for it, so ask every day. Be patient and wait on him to work out his plan.

IMPATIENCE BREEDS DOUBT

You tell yourself nothing is ever going to change, nothing is ever going to get better, and God is not going to deliver you. When you become restless and depressed over the lack of change in your situation, the door to hopelessness and depression begins to open. When this occurs, your faith becomes weakened. Feelings of doubt and despair draw you away from God, making it increasingly difficult to move forward in healing. Impatience can be a direct path to bitterness and despondency and can easily be an obstacle placed directly in front of you, blocking you from receiving a sense of peace and hope. When you are impatient, your circumstance and pain become your primary focus.

Being impatient and not trusting in God to get you through is why you so desperately seek immediate relief when you find yourself amid an unbearable circumstance. Left to your own devices, you will often dig yourself into a deeper pit of despair. You may busy yourself with excessive activities like work or exercise; try to numb the pain with alcohol or prescription medication; stay in bed and just sleep; escape with pornography; or even be tempted to check out or go into denial.

Denial is what I do. I deny the depth and reality of my truth. In my mind, if I can make it go away then I don't have to hurt so badly. I pull back and hedge myself into solitude, trying to numb myself by denying the existence of my pain. Denial is how I initially coped with my dad's indictment. I didn't allow myself to even think about the possibility of my dad going to prison. I told myself a miracle would happen, and he would not have to go. But he did go. I had to come out of my self-protected denial and face this reality to move forward.

Denial, or whatever vice you choose to try and make the pain go away, works for a while, but in the end, you have to face the truth.

Impatience can make its way into your grief, robbing you of God's limitless peace. Proverbs 13:12 states, "Hope deferred makes the heart sick." This is not God's desire for you, because he knows the consequence of hopelessness.

He fully understands the depth of your pain and wants more than anything to rescue you from your despair. Your hope comes through Christ even when you feel trapped in your grief. Being desperate in your sorrow does not condemn you to hopelessness; rather, it's like having scales on your eyes, blinding you from seeing your life through God's perspective. Trusting in God can remove these scales. You, like Joseph, have to choose to believe God has a plan even if you cannot see it until you are farther down the road.

STAYING THE COURSE

Perseverance requires a steady, persistent course of action. For me, staying the course is the most challenging part of walking through a difficult circumstance. Keeping my vision focused on God is a daily commitment. I am easily distracted, especially by the things surrounding me every day. When things are good, I feel good, but when things are bad, I feel bad. On the days I feel bad, I struggle the most. Even though I feel bad, I have to stay focused and stay on course.

Being steadfast in your circumstances and trusting that God will give you the courage to walk through whatever lies ahead of you is difficult when you feel as though you cannot go on. This is the time to follow Joseph's example. When you are in the pit, look up and look out. Being in the pit is not the time to look at your surroundings and conclude your fate. What if Joseph had failed to look beyond the pit? What would have happened if he had given up on God and had taken matters into his own hands? He would have disrupted God's plan to restore and rebuild all that was taken from him. You don't want to take matters into your own hands and give into your fears and doubt God's ability to deliver you through your sorrow. You want to be like Joseph and trust in God and stay the course.

BEING DELIVERED OUT

Being delivered out of our circumstance is what we all hope and pray for, because it is quick and immediate. When God quickly delivers you out of your circumstance, there is clear evidence of his miraculous power and mercy.

When God immediately delivered the children of Israel out of the hands of the Egyptians by parting the waters of the Red Sea, his miraculous power was on display for everyone to see. The Israelites—God's chosen people—were in immediate need of a miracle when faced with this impossible task. Instructed by God, Moses led the children of Israel out of Egypt and into the promised land. After leaving Egypt in the middle of the night, they made their escape to the promised land. When they came upon the waters of the Red Sea, they were stopped dead in their tracks. As the leader of this nation of people, Moses stood on a hilltop and raised his arms toward the heavens with his staff in hand and asked God to deliver them out!

God immediately answered by miraculously parting the roaring waters of the turbulent sea. God wanted to make it clear to everyone that he was the one and only true God. In a time where there was an abundance of idols and false gods, God wanted to demonstrate his mighty and miraculous power. When he supernaturally manifested his absolute authority over the sea by dividing the arresting waters for the Israelites to walk through, he did not want anyone to question who the God of Israel was.

Everyone was in awe of this inconceivable demonstration of God's power and authority. People shouted, praised, and worshiped him for his extraordinary hand of deliverance. Even the Egyptians were seized with fear and wonder.

There are times in life where a manifestation of God's miraculous touch is evident, and you can see God's power demonstrated right in front of you. There are times when you need a miracle, and you actually get one.

A miracle is what I needed when my husband, an OB/GYN, decided he wanted to reduce his workload so he could experience less stress and be able to spend more time at home with our children and me. Making this decision required faith. With a change of workload came a significant change in income. With this new salary, we could not afford to live in our current home, so by faith, we decided to go ahead and reduce his patient load before our house actually sold. At the time, I thought our house would sell quickly, but this did not happen. We were quickly running through our savings to pay the mortgage. Because I was so willing to give up our home, I thought God would immediately allow it to sell. Our home sat on the market for over a year. It was discouraging and difficult to make ends meet. I started to wonder if the change in my husband's workload was worth it, because the financial stress was beginning to take its toll on him.

During this time, we were leaders of a small Bible study group that had grown to approximately twenty-five families, all of whom came to our house once a month. In the home we were trying to sell, we had plenty of space for everyone, but I had no idea what we would do once we moved. They certainly would not fit in our rental property. However, I knew that God would somehow work it out for us to continue leading this Bible study; I just didn't know how.

I would never have imagined God's next move in our lives. Our contract expired with the real estate company, and we were in the process of finding another agent. After interviewing one of the most well-known Realtors in our area, my husband and I were ready to sign on the dotted line. But immediately after the Realtor left, I heard in my mind the words *"do not sign the contract."* I asked my husband if he thought God was telling me to hold off on our signatures. He said it was certainly possible. We decided to pray and ask God to confirm to both of us the route we should take. After we had prayed, we both decided to call the Realtor and decline to move forward with a formal contract. That took faith and courage! By this time, we were desperate. We had run through our savings and were unsure how to make the next mortgage payment. We needed an immediate miracle. We went to bed that night, wondering if we had done the right thing. We both reassured each other God would provide.

The next day, our home's previous owners knocked on our front door. We were shocked! They told us they were interested in purchasing their home back from us. If that wasn't miraculous enough, they offered to trade houses. They were prepared to buy our house and sell us theirs. Something like that could only come out of God's playbook.

This is a circumstance that I would call being delivered *out*. Although we walked through a year of trying to sell the house, God was waiting for the right time. When that time came, he immediately placed his favor on us, and our home sold instantly. I could have never dreamed of such a scenario.

The previous owners lived in a beautiful home down the street, perfect for us. It was small enough for us to comfortably afford the mortgage but large enough to continue our Bible study. It even had a four-car garage where we could make a playroom for all the children to play while the adults studied God's Word inside the house.

Another miracle in this story was our obedience to listen when I believed God told me not to sign that contract. By not hiring the Realtor, we were able to forgo all of the fees they would charge for selling our home. The previous owners' offer was our exact asking price minus those Realtor fees. Simply miraculous. We could only accept this offer because we were not under a contract requiring us to pay a Realtor to sell our home. God was our real-estate broker who did not charge us a penny.

All along, God had a plan. He knew where he was taking us and used this circumstance to strengthen our faith and bring him glory.

Being delivered through your heartache is part of the bigger picture, but being delivered out of it can also be a part of the bigger picture as well.

THE DANGER OF COMPLACENCY

You would think that having a miraculous encounter with God would seal your faith forever, but like anything else, over time, our memories start to fade, and so does our faith. We are fickle. When we encounter a miraculous touch from God, it is easy to see his power and goodness in our lives, but with the distance of time and heartache, we soon forget how great God is.

This is exactly what happened to the Israelites. It was not long after the miracle of the Red Sea that they started complaining and turning their back on God altogether. Why? Their memory had started to fade, and there had been no transformation in their lives. After their miraculous escape, the Israelites failed to walk in a relationship with God. Their lack of intimacy with God left them irritable and discontent, making it easier to turn their back on him. Often, you become complacent and quickly forget about his goodness when you fail to engage in an intimate relationship with God after receiving a supernatural deliverance from your pain. That is, until the next painful event in your life. A lack of transformation will often lead to spiritual indifference and complacency.

Becoming complacent is why, I believe, God may choose to deliver individuals through rather than out of their circumstances. God wants to see lives transformed.

THE POWER OF TRANSFORMATION

Not everyone who is delivered directly out of their circumstance will become complacent and lose faith in God's ability to deliver them again, but this is typically what happens without transformation.

The Israelites lost faith after they were delivered out of the hands of the Egyptians. They failed to walk in a relationship with God— they did not experience the power of a transformed heart. Because they were delivered immediately out of their circumstance, they did not go through a refining process. God chose to deliver the Israelites immediately out of their hardship to demonstrate his great power. He wanted his children and the Egyptians to know, without a doubt, that he was the only one and true God. After such a mighty illustration of his power, I am sure everyone who witnessed it was in awe of God and convinced of his holiness and authority.

There are times when God wants you to understand and embrace his power and see his glory in the miracle, but that does not mean he does not want to see your life transformed.

God is the same yesterday, today, and forever. He is still in the business of performing miracles. When you trust in his sovereignty—his ability to make decisions regarding the fate of your life based on his divine capacity to see things you cannot see—God will transform your heart.

Whether you are being delivered immediately out or being delivered through, God seeks for you to have a transformed heart. Transformation changes your perception. Rarely do you have control over your circumstance, but you always have control over the ability to change your beliefs and ideas about the unexpected events in your life. Being able to have a different perspective is the power of transformation! When you see things as God sees them, you are no longer at the mercy of your circumstance. With God's help, you can rise above your heartache and suffering and receive God's supernatural peace.

Being in prison taught Joseph humility, trust in God, and how to have peace and contentment in the face of adversity. His hardships, heartaches, and trials transformed his heart into a compassionate, humble, and wise leader. Likewise, my dad's transformation in prison was life changing as well.

A NEW MAN

Before my dad was indicted for mail fraud, his desire to succeed by the world's standards drove his behavior and priorities. He worked hard, never missing a day at the office in over thirty years, arriving early, staying late, and doing whatever it took to get the job done. He was absorbed, preoccupied, and consumed with his work. Sure, God was important, but not necessarily essential to his daily life. He was saved, he went to church and tithed, but he did not experience Christ as his personal friend. He did not believe he needed Christ in that way. My dad thought he was self-sufficient, independent, and capable. ⁙

The day my dad was sentenced, he realized he could not walk this path alone. He asked us to send him only books and commentaries about the Bible for him to read. He used his time of incarceration to shut himself off from the world, to seek truth, and get to know Christ intimately. When my dad came home from prison, work was no longer his priority. All he could talk about were the things he learned through reading God's Word. Most times, he wept when talking about these truths. The first thing he does each morning now is read the Bible, pray, and listen to worship music. There have been many mornings where I have witnessed him weeping as he read God's Word. He is no longer in a hurry to get somewhere to do this deal or to finish that contract. He hangs around family gatherings until we are all ready to leave. We never saw this kind of calm and peace in him until after his time in prison.

Seeing this change in my dad changed all of us. It was inspiring to see such a strong, self-sufficient man become so tender to the ways of God. My dad is not the same man because of what he went through. He is kinder, more patient, more present, and more loving. He learned how to have a personal relationship with Christ and surrendered his heart to him in every aspect of his life. My dad taught us about the importance and power of love. I learned I could walk through painful circumstances with Christ by my side. God chose to deliver all of us through this painful experience, not miraculously out of it; but in the journey, all of us received an unexpected transformation.

FOCUS ON THE RIGHT THING

When you encounter heartache or adversity, you are faced with the choice to accept your reality with the possibility of change or run from it. Sometimes you have to live in the tension between these two. Acceptance does not mean approval of your circumstances. It means you allow pain into your life, not because you want it there, but because pain is a part of grief and working through your grief makes you stronger. God sees your pain much differently than you do. He sees the power your struggles can have to change your life and transform your heart. Being delivered through or delivered out should not be your focus. God is your focus. His grace and mercy are what will see you either immediately out of your pain or patiently through it.

Being delivered out is what we pray for, and what we hope will happen. We all want to see a grand demonstration of God's power. But often, like the Israelites, being delivered out of our circumstances is not always the best thing. Only a sovereign God can know the course that our lives will take. If you are delivered immediately out of your hardship as the Israelites were, be careful not to take your healing for granted by losing your focus and becoming complacent in your relationship with God like the Israelites did. Going through a process of healing like Joseph may be difficult and challenging, but you will have the opportunity to learn more about who you are, who God is, and what your purpose here on this earth is. Keeping your eyes on him and remaining focused on transformation will keep you on God's sovereign path for your life.

GOD'S TIMING

To question God about his timing can also create doubt and uncertainty. Doubt breeds impatience and discontentment, hindering your ability to expand your vision to see your circumstances through the lens of Christ. He sees your future; he knows the end result, and it is up to you to trust in him to see you through. When you are irritable and discontent, it is difficult to see or feel anything other than your pain. To move from doubt to certainty in God's truth, you have to trust in who he is. God is holy, loving, and faithful. He will see you through. You have to be patient and persevere through your circumstances by believing and trusting in the nature of God, knowing the journey will create purpose in your pain.

Whether being delivered out or through, remember God determines the timeline. Being patient and allowing God to walk with you through your hardship and sorrow will give you the strength to face each day. In his perfect timing, you will be able to move beyond your grief and find purpose in your pain.

When you put timelines and expectations on your healing, you become restless and impatient. When you are frustrated and discontent, it is easy to miss opportunities for refinement during the journey. But accepting God's timing as the best timing will allow you the freedom to walk through the healing process one day, one step at a time. God promises he will give you enough grace, courage, and strength to move through each moment of each day with hope.

Many times you do not get served exactly what you want or what you believe you deserve, but God knows what you need. His answers may not look like you thought they would, but when you pull back and look through his expanded lens, you are assured he is working out the details of your life in a supernatural way. Often these answers go far beyond anything you could have ever imagined. Sometimes an instant change will occur, and other times it is gradual. Both have their place in your life, but God, in his infinite wisdom, knows which path is the right one for you to travel. His plan always includes a method of finding purpose and meaning in your pain. Regardless of how God chooses to deliver you, hope is what will carry you through.

HELPFUL TOOLS

1. Find solace and peace in connecting with God through prayer.
2. Be grateful. Appreciate the good things, the small things, the beautiful things that surround you even in the middle of tragedy and heartache.
3. Trust God sees the bigger picture. He is working things out behind the scenes to deliver you through your suffering and grief.
4. Be patient and trust God has a plan. Persevere and stay the course, even on days when the pain seems too great.
5. Change your perspective. Step back and see things as God sees them. Put on the expanded lens of Christ.

6. Be willing to make changes in your life. To move forward in your grief, you have to be open to transformation. God wants to transform your heart, mind, and soul to be more like him.

7. Keep your focus on God, not on your circumstance.

8. Do the next thing. Do not become overwhelmed with thoughts of where you think you need to be in your recovery. Simply focus your attention on doing whatever is next. Once you have accomplished that task, then do the next one. One day and one minute at a time.

9. Accept completely the circumstances that surround your grief and heartache. Don't fight them. Though you badly want things to change, accept them for what they are and understand things may look different over time. Accept that God's timing often looks different from ours. Look for ways to find meaning and purpose in your suffering.

Part Two

Drinking the Cup

3

A Cup of Despair
How to Change Your Perception

$\mathcal{I}$ had been happily married for five years. Like most little girls, I dreamed about growing up and marrying a prince. I imagined myself living in a beautiful home with a stately front yard and a wooden planked swing tied to an old towering oak tree swaying back and forth while two or three children playfully romped around in the picturesque surroundings. Standing in the breeze, I saw myself thoroughly captivated by their innocence and their beauty while they played.

That's not asking too much, is it?

As children, we all have dreams we hope will one day become a reality, but sadly life does not always play out as we had hoped. Today, my childhood imagery makes me smile considering its innocence, but when I contemplate this dream through the lens of reality, it makes me tilt my head downward and simply shake it back and forth. As a child, the thought of having a loving husband with three adorable children and living in a beautiful home would be the ideal life. It did not seem too much to ask for, to believe in—to hope the dream would someday be real.

Though I had to wait longer than I wanted, my childhood dreams started to become a reality. Everything seemed perfect! I was married to a handsome doctor, I had two beautiful children who kept me busy at home, I was a volunteer at Junior League, and I taught a women's Bible study at my church. I even had a charming homemade swing tied to an impressive pecan tree in the front of my yard. Life was full and happy; I couldn't ask for anything more. I would often think how lucky I was to have such a wonderful husband, beautiful children, and a blessed life. My hopes and dreams were coming true until one unexpected day, my idyllic life shattered.

Initially, I had a sense something was not right. I brushed it off, telling myself it was nothing—but was it?

My husband, Jeff, had recently lost his mom and could not seem to move through his grief. He appeared sad all the time, so he agreed to see a therapist to help him manage his depression. I was relieved to know he was willing to see someone who could help him work through this difficult season in his life. I tried to pretend everything was not as it was because I did not want the dream to end. It was too perfect.

Then the day came when I woke up, and the dream was over. A nightmare ensued in its place. I was in the kitchen making dinner while my children played under my feet when the phone rang. It was my husband's therapist. He had asked her to call and share some shocking news that he was too ashamed to tell me himself. She warned I might find it difficult to hear. When I heard the words "addiction" come out of her mouth, my world stopped. I couldn't breathe. Her voice started echoing on the other end of the phone; I slowly slid myself down the side of the counter, dropping the receiver onto the floor.

When I was in graduate school, one of the classes I was required to take as a student in the counseling program was addiction and recovery. This class was my least favorite. I had no interest. I was annoyed at having to take this course, thinking it was a ridiculous requirement since this was not the area of counseling I was pursuing. I considered it a waste of my time. But, despite my disdain, I dutifully took the class.

Having completed this course, I had a pretty good understanding of addiction. The class further confirmed my lack of interest and desire to work within this field of counseling. I learned that individuals with addictions can be resistant to treatment, and the prognosis for recovery is often not a good one. It was depressing. Not having any experience personally or professionally with addictions, I believed I had nothing to offer anyone struggling to overcome addictive behaviors.

After taking the required class, I was left with the notion that addiction is a treatment-resistant, emotionally painful, and debilitating illness often with devastating consequences. I remember my professor saying, "Once an addict, always an addict."

Living with addiction as part of the equation was not the life I dreamed of, nor was it the gritty kind of life I ever thought I would live.

Sitting limp on the floor with my knees tightly tucked underneath me, I felt sick. I thought to myself, *This cannot be happening to me—not this, not addiction.*

How? I thought. *How did this happen?* Recalling the last several months and considering Jeff's family history, the pieces started to fall into place. Surgery for his foot, painkillers; the unexpected death of his mother, painkillers; depression, more painkillers. His mom was an addict and an alcoholic, his stepdad an alcoholic, his brother who died by suicide an alcoholic. My heart sank. The picture was clear. How could I have been so naive?

For Jeff, I learned that what one pill every few hours would cure, now took five or six. He was not taking the medication for pain; he took this medicine for a sense of well-being. He wanted to feel normal. Getting up every morning, he would begin his day, hoping he would feel better. When hopelessness and depression took over, though, he would take the prescription medication to dull the emotional pain—again and again throughout the day. This pattern of behavior became a vicious cycle he could not seem to break. When I had asked him if he was still taking medication from his surgery, he lied, telling me he was not taking anything. I wanted to believe him even though, deep down, I knew things were not fine. He confidently told me he felt okay—maybe a little depressed, but otherwise, he was fine. His feeling fine was far from the truth. Everything was not fine. He later told me he would pray every day for God to help him not take another pill. Every day he failed.

Shortly after that disturbing phone call, I called a treatment center in a panic. Talking so fast, I could barely keep up with my own words; I desperately pleaded for them to send someone to our home to talk to my husband. Within two hours, a man and a woman showed up at our doorstep. It felt like a whirlwind. A few hours earlier, I had been preparing dinner and watching my children beneath me play with their toys on the gray tiled floor like I did most days. Life was normal. Now I was watching professionals conduct an intervention on my husband in our living room. I felt overwhelmed. I questioned myself. *Did I react too quickly? Maybe we could have worked this out. What have I done?*

These two individuals convinced Jeff and me he needed help—professional help. I frantically packed him a suitcase, and within an hour of them arriving at our home, they drove away with my husband shamefully tucked into the back seat of their car. They headed to the airport to fly to a treatment facility in the Texas hill country. He would be more than eight hours away for an extended amount of time while I was left alone with a toddler and a preschooler to somehow keep our lives from unraveling more than it already had. I would have to tell the hospital and his colleagues that he would not be returning to work, and that he was addicted to hydrocodone. If his employer terminated him, I would have to decide how to handle the finances and pay for treatment. It would be up to me to manage the chaos and figure out how we would live with the shame of him being a doctor practicing medicine while on drugs. My thoughts and to-do list were pulsating in my head. I felt ashamed and foolish for not knowing what was happening right in front of me. The truth was banging in my thoughts: *I am married to a drug addict.*

The perfect world in which I had lived had instantly turned into a scandal. The beautiful house, the comfortable lifestyle, the pedestal on which I had placed my husband did not define my life anymore. My life was now defined by chaos, deceit, addiction, and shame.

While I watched the two intervention specialists drive my husband away, I deliberately leaned back onto the door frame of my house, contemplating the sequence of events that had just transpired. In what seemed like a blink of an eye, the course of my life had dramatically changed. Wanting to feel comfort, I gently pulled my one-year-old daughter tighter onto my hip while my older son grabbed onto my leg. Not wanting to cry in front of my children, I just stood there for what seemed an eternity. My head started to spin, and I felt faint and weak at my knees. I was flooded with depressing thoughts: *Jeff is not the right man for me, I made the wrong choice, Jeff is not the man I thought he was, I don't want this life, I can't trust him, I should have seen the warning signs, this is not the life I want, I want out—no I want to die.* Not knowing what else to do, I turned around and walked back into the shadows of what once was and would never be again. I put my babies into their beds and then collapsed across mine and cried myself to sleep, hoping I would never wake up.

POWER OF PERCEPTION

It is rare when life turns out exactly the way you expect. Disappointments often hang over you like the threat of rain on a cloudy day. You anticipated life's goodness, but instead, life served the unexpected and the unwanted. Everything is moving along normally when out of nowhere you are faced with the unforeseen, the unimaginable—a swift and jolting change, of course. Your circumstances take you hostage emotionally, leaving you with feelings of despair and hopelessness.

What do you do when life lets you down, when disappointments cloud your ability to see the possibilities that may lie ahead, when the unforeseen happens and life as you know it abruptly comes to an end? You are suddenly in the wake of devastation, asking yourself a barrage of questions you have no idea how to answer: *How do I pick up the pieces? How do I move beyond the pain? How do I take another step?* It's like being in a pitch-black room trying to find the door. You put your hands in front of you, swiping them up and down and side to side through the air, hoping to touch a wall that will lead you to the exit. You are gripped with fear, anxiety, and a sense of doom because you can only see black, and you can't feel anything but air. You think, *Maybe there is no door, there is no escape.* Your feelings of fear and hopelessness taint your perception of what could be despite your circumstances.

Perception is how you identify the events in your life and make sense of them through your senses. You see, you feel, you hear, then you draw a conclusion about your experience. It is through your perceptions that you create your reality. This is why two people can experience the same event but describe completely different accounts of the incident.

When you have an experience, you will have an initial judgment about what just happened based on what you think you saw, heard, and felt. Once you have conceptualized a perceived idea about your encounter, you will have feelings about that event. Feelings can range from joy and excitement to fear and hopelessness depending on your perception and interpretation of what just happened. Finally, you react and engage in behaviors that represent your perceptions, thoughts, and feelings.

Experience→Perception→Thoughts→Feelings→Behaviors

The way you perceive the world and everything around you directly affects your thoughts, feelings, and behaviors. This type of perception is referred to as top-down processing. Your expectations from previous experiences influence your perceptions of what is currently happening. You use the information already in your head to perceive or make sense of what you see, hear, or feel. In top-down processing, information moves down from your preconceived ideas to your external thoughts and behaviors in a top to bottom motion.

For example, most of my clients in my counseling practice suffered from post-traumatic stress and depression due to some sort of trauma. Based on their prior experiences, many of them had a preconceived idea that the world they lived in was evil. However, not everyone would agree with my clients' perspectives. Some see the world as basically good and humankind as generally honest and law-abiding. Both groups of people live in the same world but have very different perceptions based upon their past experiences.

The group that sees the world as "bad" will often be pessimistic about life. This viewpoint can affect their ability to trust other people and believe good can come from their circumstances. The other group that considers the world to be "good" may have a more positive outlook on life in general but may be naive in situations where they should be more cautious. Both groups have preconceived ideas about the world that influence their perception of the circumstances they encounter.

I remember one client in particular who had been physically abused and abandoned by her father. She had this "tough girl" exterior around her. She believed it was up to her to protect herself from other people regardless of who they were. Now, as an adult, she was afraid of being hurt and abandoned by someone she loved. Her fears hindered her ability to manage relationships successfully, and her perception of others interfered with her capacity to become vulnerable and trusting. Because her father mistreated her and left without a word of explanation, she was determined to protect herself. Her mother, however, was her source of comfort and stability, but when she died, my client's world, as she knew it, fell apart. She was consumed by grief. This circumstance is what brought her to me. Her mother's death confirmed, in her mind, that people you love either hurt you or leave you. This preconceived bias hindered her from forming new relationships with others. She concluded it was better to protect herself than risk being hurt or abandoned. This viewpoint left her depressed and alone.

Your perceptions will reinforce your existing ideas and beliefs or contradict them, similar to my client. My client believed the people she loved would leave her, so she kept them at arm's length. Her mother dying confirmed her belief in abandonment.

When your beliefs are reinforced, they become more substantial, like evidence used by a prosecuting attorney to sway a jury during a court trial. When deliberations occur, the evidence will support the prosecuting attorney's case, making it unlikely for the jurors to side with the defendant. The evidence supports the prosecutor's theory, making it unlikely that the mind of the jurors would change. Likewise, when your perception of an event reinforces an existing idea or belief, the probability of your values and beliefs changing is unlikely. Your perceptions act like the evidence given in a trial. They confirm what you already thought to be true.

Think of perception as a glass window. When the glass is clear and clean of any smudges or debris, you can see through it perfectly. Nothing distorts the view, but if the window is cloudy, obstructed, or smeared with dirt, your ability to see through it is significantly impaired. The smudges, obstructions, and dirt represent preconceived ideas, and the inability to see clearly represents your perceptions. When your window is dirty, your perception of what you think you are seeing becomes tainted, but your perception is clear and precise when your window is clean. It is like looking out a dirty window and thinking you see a monster, but when you clean off the dirt, in reality, you see a tree.

Preconceived Ideas→Experience→Perception→Thoughts→ Feelings→Behaviors

Your perception will warp when events unfold with a preconceived idea based not on truth but on a particular bias. These prior judgments blemish the truth about your experience. They cloud your ability to see reality accurately. Consequently, your thoughts, feelings, and reactions toward your current and future encounters are acutely affected.

The process of perception functions much like a filter. Imagine a filter that is shaped like a funnel. It is wide at the top and narrows at the bottom. The wide opening makes it easy to pour in liquid at the top. The narrow opening at the bottom will prevent anything large and unwanted from escaping. The point of the filter is to take out any impurities, ensuring the contents leaving the filter will be clean and purified. However, if the filter is damaged or defective, the contents that come out of the bottom will be contaminated.

Think of this system in terms of mental processing. You readily take information into your mental filter from whatever you are experiencing. Your thoughts and perceptions will act as a strainer. They will filter your experiences as they pass through. You will hold on to what you perceive to be true and discard what you believe to be distortions of the truth. Think of making coffee. Before you can strain coffee grounds through a coffee maker, you have to put in one of those white bowl-like paper filters. This filter keeps the coffee grounds out of your coffee. Without it, your coffee would turn into mush. Our minds work a lot like a coffee maker. If we fail to put in a clean, crisp filter, then our thoughts and beliefs will turn into mush.

To have a clean filter, you have to be clear on what you believe to be true about God. His Word and his character are like the paper filter you use to remove the coffee grounds. You analyze your experience against the truth of God's Word and through the nature of his character. When you experience heartache and loss, hope comes from the purified filter of God's truth. However, a filter that has been contaminated by past hurts, preconceived ideas, fears, shame, unforgiveness, or familial and historic messaging, will pollute your perceptions and beliefs about your circumstances. Polluted perceptions change what you think you hear, see, and feel, profoundly impacting your thoughts, feelings, and behaviors. When your perceptions are not filtered with the truth, you end up thinking and believing a flawed version of your circumstance.

Perceptions have a substantial impact on how you view your experiences. Your views can be positive or negative based on your filter. However, if your filter has been flawed or damaged, then your perceptions will be flawed as well. Again, think of seeing a monster instead of a tree. If your filter is contaminated, it will distort what you think you see, but when your filter has been purified, you will understand what you are seeing is not a monster but a tree. Faulty beliefs and harmful past experiences will damage and taint your perceptions. A tarnished filter will be unable to accurately determine what is true or not, but when you cleanse your filter with the Word of God, you will see your circumstances from his perspective, not your own.

My perception of addiction set the stage for me to have feelings of despair and hopelessness. Because of the historical message I had received in my training of an addict's low probability of recovery, my perception of what my life would look like for my children and me was severely tainted. I had decided addiction meant chaos, emotional bankruptcy, continued deceit, repeated failures, and financial ruin. Although my perception was based on scientific research, it was not based on the truth of God's Word. During my training, the information I had gathered clouded my belief that God could intervene and create a different path. I failed to filter my experience through the truth of God's Word. Instead, I screened my circumstance against worldly knowledge, which warped my perception of what I thought was truth. This perception had a profound effect on my thoughts, my feelings, and my behavior.

A SHARED LOSS

In the Old Testament book of Ruth, two unsuspecting women show us how perception can play a significant role within unexpected circumstances. As Ruth and Naomi's story unfolds, we see firsthand its powerful impact. The two women walked through the same tragedy and hardships, with very different points of view.

Naomi was Ruth's mother-in-law, who was a strong woman of faith. She grew up in a Jewish home and married a man who loved God as much as she did. They had two sons. Together, Naomi and her husband, Elimelek, raised their sons to fear and love God. When their boys grew older, an unanticipated famine swept across their land, depleting their community with the accessibility to obtain food. Desperate to find provision, they determined they had no other choice but to flee their home in Bethlehem. They moved to Moab, approximately sixty miles east of their homeland. This was a bold move because the Moabites and the Israelites were enemies and frequently in conflict. Their moving to Moab gives us a clue into how desperate they were.

While living in this foreign city, Naomi's boys grew into men and married two Moabite women named Ruth and Orpah, neither of whom shared the same faith in God as they did. Despite their disbelief, Naomi took them in as her own; she loved them and wanted them to understand who God was and why she and her sons so faithfully served him. Naomi taught Ruth and Orpah everything she knew about her God. Ruth listened intently to every word her mother-in-law said, not just listening but also watching, learning, and believing. With her heart changed and her mind transformed, Ruth took on Naomi's faith and believed in God. She chose to believe and have faith because of Naomi's endearing love for her and Naomi's commitment to teaching her the true nature and character of God.

Then the unexpected and unthinkable happened—death. First, Naomi's husband died, leaving her with her two boys; then ten years later, both of her sons died unexpectedly. These three women were suddenly widows with no means to support themselves. In this ancient society, women had no legal or economic rights to own land or have any resources to make a living. Naomi, Ruth, and Orpah had lost the protection and support of their husbands, making them vulnerable to immense poverty.

These three women, no longer wives of working men, suddenly found themselves homeless, with no stability or status in their community. They essentially lost all they had. Naomi made the difficult decision to leave the home she had created with her husband and two sons to return to her people in Bethlehem with nothing to call her own. Naomi believed she was destined to suffer for the rest of her life, and she did not want Ruth and Orpah to have the same destiny of poverty and despair as her, so she pleaded with them to stay in Moab. Naomi thought both Ruth and Oprah would have a better chance at rebuilding their lives in their own homeland.

However, Ruth could not bear to be separated from Naomi. Regardless of the hardship they would have to face, Ruth was not willing to leave her mother-in-law. She was prepared to leave her home and follow Naomi to build a new life in a foreign land with no guarantee of security or provision. As the story continues to unfold, you can begin to get a glimpse into the different perceptions of Ruth and Naomi. Naomi was convinced her life would be bitter and distressing with no hope of a viable future. Ruth, on the other hand, was hopeful. She believed the God whom Naomi talked about would not only provide for them but deliver them out of their despair.

FAITH PUT TO THE TEST

"My husband is dead, and so are my sons! God, why would you do this to me?" I can hear Naomi's desperate cries echoing in my mind. Naomi had dedicated her life to serving God, her husband, and her sons. She had poured her heart and soul into teaching Ruth and Orpah about God's love and faithfulness. But the unforeseen loss of her two sons put Naomi's faith to the test.

There was no Bible sitting on the coffee table for someone to read. Everything known about God was learned through the spoken word, gained by firsthand experience, or taught by the priest reading the Torah in the temple. Ruth's only means of knowing God came from hearing Naomi talk about him and watching her live for him. I can imagine Ruth listening to Naomi talk about the faithfulness of God when he delivered the Israelites from slavery. Ruth probably hung on Naomi's every word when she described the night the Israelites escaped and the glorious miracle of them crossing the Red Sea, all while the two of them kneaded dough and baked bread.

When tragedy struck, however, God's faithfulness was called into question. The looming interrogation of *why* haunted Naomi, challenging her beliefs in a loving and faithful God. The life she had worked so hard to build was stripped from her in what seemed like an instant. Her life had collapsed, and almost overnight, she had become homeless and destitute with no family to help her. How could this be God's plan? Why would God take her husband and both sons? Naomi could not see past her pain and her dire circumstance. All she could see was heartache and despair. Naomi was angry. She felt resentful and betrayed. So betrayed that she changed her name to Mara, which means bitter. Changing her name indicated God's betrayal and abandonment. She believed God was responsible for her tragic set of circumstances. Naomi blamed God for taking the life of her husband and sons, leaving her alone and destitute. Her perception of her future had become bleak and hopeless.

A DAMAGED FILTER

From the outside looking in, we begin to see what is happening in Naomi's mind. She had already had a traumatic experience early in her marriage when famine struck. She had to leave her family and friends unexpectedly. She quickly gathered her two young boys and what little items she could carry to follow her husband. Naomi had to start over creating a different life in a foreign land. After she made herself a new home and her boys grow into men, she experienced another tragic loss—the death of her husband. These two experiences most likely affected her mental filter through top-down processing. Remember, in top-down processing, your expectations from previous experiences influence your perceptions of what is currently happening. This information from the past is used to make sense of your present circumstance. You essentially draw a conclusion about your current situation based on your past experiences. In top-down processing, information moves down from your preconceived ideas based on your past into your external thoughts and behaviors. The top-down processing of Naomi's past experience affected her perception of her latest tragedy.

Because of the two heartbreaking losses in Naomi's past, her filter was probably faulty. When her boys died, she may have perceived her circumstance as evidence her future was doomed. Due to her previous losses, she may have thought, *That's it; I am destined to be cursed by God.* This thought filtered through her earlier experiences of separation and death. These tragedies confirmed in her mind that nothing good was going to happen in her life. She believed misfortune and hardship were to be her fate. Naomi failed to filter her circumstance against the truth of God's Word. She allowed her previous experiences to dictate her perception of her future, leaving her with feelings of despair and hopelessness. She saw things from her perspective rather than God's.

Ruth, on the other hand, did not share the same despair as Naomi. Though she was devastated by her loss, her choices indicated she was not without hope. Ruth told Naomi she was committed to her and her God. Because she had faith in Naomi's God, she was willing to leave her family and home behind. She courageously decided to walk alongside Naomi despite Naomi's bitterness and rejection of God's unforeseen plan for their lives. In Ruth 1:16–17 she told Naomi, "Do not press me to leave you or to turn back from following you! Where you go, I will go; where you lodge, I will lodge; your people shall be my people, and your God my God. Where you die, I will die—there will I be buried" (NRSV).

Simply put, Ruth had faith in God. She believed in the stories she heard Naomi tell her of God's power to deliver his children. Ruth trusted in God's promise to be Jehovah Jireh, their provider, just like he was for the Israelites in the wilderness. Ruth's perception of her future was filtered through God's truth and promises. Her perception of God's nature produced a belief that solidified her initial perception regarding her circumstance. Her confidence in God's faithfulness to bring purpose to her pain and provide provision for her future shaped her thoughts, beliefs, and behaviors.

Naomi, however, had lost faith in God. She believed God had forgotten and abandoned her. Ruth was full of hope. Naomi was bitter and beaten down. Ruth was ready to start a new life. Naomi was barely hanging on to the life she had. What made the difference for these two women? Perception.

SEEING AS GOD SEES

Seeing as God sees makes me think of the difference between seeing an awesome movie on a little black and white TV or in full color on a big screen with three-dimensional technology. It also makes me think of going to Disney World.

My family loved going to Disney World, where things seem so full of color and adventure. We liked to go in the wintertime, because there weren't as many people at the park, and we were impatient when it came to long lines. We'd rather put up with the cooler weather than wait in lines and get elbowed by crowds of people. We're awed by all the special effects, especially the 3-D adventures everywhere in the parks. The 3-D productions give us such incredible experiences, more than we could ever get on a little TV or even in a movie theater.

When you walk into a 3-D show or ride at any of the Disney parks, you're handed a set of 3-D glasses. If you don't wear the glasses, you can't fully experience the special effects of the adventure. But when you put them on, everything changes. The clarity is stunning. Characters will often jump out at you, and the scenery tingles with color, scent, and texture. All the plants, trees, rivers, and sky fly off the screen, causing you to feel as though you are actually standing amid the scene. I recently went on the Pandora ride in Animal Kingdom and could not believe what I saw and experienced wasn't real. I was immediately swept into the adventure and became part of the story. I honestly felt like I had been transported into another world. It was invigorating to experience the views and perspective I would otherwise have never been able to experience had I not been wearing those special 3-D glasses.

This is how it is when you have supernatural clarity. When you put on the lens of Christ, you can filter out all the things that are not true and do not make sense. His lens gives you a crystal-clear vision of the things he wants you to see. His Word comes alive with the truth you may have otherwise missed. When you see as he does, when you enter into his presence, your perception changes. You are awakened. You see and understand things you couldn't before. You read a passage of scripture that becomes more than words; they become living words. Like in the 3-D movie, they jump off the page and brush up against you, shining a light into a dark place, giving you comfort during times of sorrow and direction when you feel lost. You have discernment that wasn't there, and your circumstances take on a different meaning. You have hope and peace in the midst of your storm. Through the lens of Christ, you can find and receive healing and comfort, peace, and love. Your point of view is bigger. You become part of the true story you are meant to live. But you cannot see as God sees unless you put on the glasses. Putting on the glasses to see as God sees comes from reading your Bible, spending time in prayer, entering into worship through singing and meditation, and surrounding yourself with other believers who will support, encourage, and pray with you.

Ruth found a way to see things as God saw them. Naomi did not, and neither did I. Naomi and I failed to see as God sees in both of our circumstances. He had a bigger plan, a purpose, a blessing, but we did not see it—we were both full of fear, dread, and despair.

THE GLASS DOES NOT HAVE TO BE HALF EMPTY

The key to accepting your disappointments and tragedies as part of God's bigger plan rather than as hopeless disasters is in how you choose to perceive them. Once you allow your perception to line up with God's bigger plan, you can see your circumstance from a different point of view. Consider the comparison of viewing a situation as a glass half full or a glass half empty. To see it as half full requires supernatural strength, especially in situations involving heartbreaking loss. The path to healing involves hope—hope that you can live again with joy and peace, hope that your life will continue to have meaning and purpose, hope your memories will bring you comfort rather than pain. Seeing your circumstance as dire and hopeless is considering the glass half empty. Both glasses have the same amount of liquid, but the perspective is different. Seeing as God sees will help you understand there is hope even in the midst of your pain.

Naomi was hopeless. In her mind, there was no one to deliver her and Ruth from their grave circumstance. She and Ruth were living day by day, not knowing where they would get their next meal. Naomi urged Ruth to go out and glean barley from the fields being harvested. Gleaning the fields was a common practice for the poor during these times. Some of the grain was allowed to fall to the ground by the farmers so impoverished people could gather what they needed for provision. Israelite law also required the corners of the fields not to be harvested. The purpose of the law was to feed the poor, the orphans, the widows, and the foreigners. It served as a safety net and resource. As they were both widows with no means to support themselves, Ruth gleaned the fields for barley. What Naomi did not know was that God had a plan! God orchestrated for Ruth to glean the field of a distant relative—a kinsman-redeemer.

In the Old Testament, a kinsman-redeemer was a male next of kin who had the privilege or responsibility to act on behalf of a relative in trouble, danger, or need. Naomi learned Ruth had been gathering barley in the field of a wealthy man named Boaz who happened to be a distant relative of the family—a male next of kin. Though distant, he was the closest relative; he was Ruth's kinsman-redeemer. Boaz was God's provision—a confirmation to Ruth God would provide. Because of a damaged filter, Naomi believed God had abandoned her and condemned her to a lonely, desolate life. She was consumed with anger, hopelessness, and fear. Her perception of God was not at all representative of who he was. She saw God as heartless and distant. She perceived him as a God of betrayal.

Ruth, on the other hand, saw God from a completely different perspective. Ruth did not have any doubt that God was going to provide for them. Her perception of God was good. She believed he was their healer, sustainer, and provider, no matter the circumstance. Even though their life did not look anything like they thought it would, her faith did not waver. She firmly believed God had a plan despite their tragedy. It was a plan of hope and redemption. Unlike Naomi's belief in an absent God, Ruth believed God was fully present.

God supernaturally and thoughtfully maneuvered Ruth's and Boaz's paths to cross. Because Ruth believed in the divine character and nature of God, she did not react to her loss with bitterness and grief as Naomi did. Her faith in God gave her hope that God would be her redeemer. Ruth saw her glass as half full. Naomi, unfortunately, viewed hers as half empty. She had a warped perception of God's character. Naomi's past hurts and trauma contaminated her filter, tainting her perception of God and his ability to provide for her.

Can you see how the difference in perception changes what you believe to be possible? Ruth filtered her tragedy through what she knew to be true about God. This truth helped her to have hope—hope that God had a bigger plan. Naomi failed to filter her past experience and her current tragedy through God's truth. She used her own logic. She used her circumstances as evidence that God did not care and was not concerned about her future. Unlike Ruth, Naomi did not see things from God's perspective. She did not believe God was Jehovah Jireh, her provider.

Examining this story from a psychological perspective demonstrates how powerful perception can be. When you look in the rearview mirror, it is easy to see how Ruth and Naomi's different perceptions affected their thoughts, feelings, and behaviors. Both of them walked through the same trauma, but both had different perceptions of their experience. Ruth had hope, and Naomi did not. As we see the drama of their lives unfold, we have the benefit of seeing the end result, but they did not. It was individually up to them to decide where they would put their faith. Naomi could have spared herself a great deal of fear, hopelessness, and despair if she had followed Ruth's lead by trusting God was in control and could see the bigger picture. Because she could not see the hand of God working, Naomi failed to believe God had a plan; but Ruth believed God was in control even though she could not see him moving.

God intervened in both of their lives in the same way despite their differences. God is full of grace. He has a plan and executes his plan even when we fail to trust him. So many times, we put ourselves through more heartache and grief because of a broken filter lined with fear, anger, and bitterness. Having a damaged filter taints God's truth, making it difficult to see things as he does. Naomi's fear, unresolved grief, and bitterness tainted her perception of God. Ruth, on the other hand, perceived her circumstances differently. Her perception of God was one of a savior and a healer. She believed he would provide for her and Naomi the same way he provided manna for the children of Israel. This perception of God brought hope and comfort to Ruth.

This story ends with Ruth and Boaz getting married and Ruth giving birth to a son who was in the direct lineage of Christ. Wow! God knew the end result. He had a masterful plan.

A BEND IN THE ROAD

When you have been hit by an unexpected tragedy, your perceptions play a decisive role in your beliefs, feelings, and reactions about what happened, about God, and about yourself. When a faulty filter distorts your perception of truth, a bend in the road becomes a roadblock, a complete change of course, or a turn in the wrong direction. When you perceive your situation as bleak and do not believe in God's ability to intervene, you are like Naomi—hopeless and bitter toward God for not stepping in. You see things exactly as they are, not what they could be.

When my life took a drastic turn in what I thought was the wrong direction, I believed God could not intervene because Jeff, not me, had decided to use drugs. How could God change the free will of my husband? I honestly believed addiction was bigger than God. My circumstance, in my mind, was not just a bend in the road; it was a definite roadblock. I thought I could not move forward.

Shortly after my husband left for treatment, I had some friends come over to pray with me. We had been friends for many years. They had been my youth pastors growing up and transitioned into friends when I married. They sat and talked with me for what seemed like hours discussing my tainted perception of God's inability to make a difference in my situation. They asked to lay hands on me as they prayed, so I let them put their hands on my shoulders, thinking it would not make a difference. But something happened in my heart as they were praying. God changed my beliefs and perceptions about who he was. I felt his presence within me so warm, so reassuring, so loving. My thoughts became clear. I was no longer confused—I understood. God was making it evident that he would never leave my husband or me and this circumstance was not the end of my journey in my marriage. It was just a bend in the road.

I could hear him say, *"Trust me, trust my Word, I will make this crooked path straight."* It was like looking at a 3-D image. I had clarity unlike I had ever had before. Scriptures I had learned as a child were jumping into my mind with such transparency and precision. I felt a brush of his presence next to me, bringing me such comfort in a time of absolute despair. I kept hearing the phrase *"This is a bend in the road."* With God's help, I started believing I could move forward on the road in front of me that abruptly turned into a direction I did not expect. Through the lens of God, I could see a purpose, a plan, and hope that our lives would not be destined for heartache and despair. Proverbs 3:5–6 gave me the confidence to know God was working on my behalf behind the scenes: "Trust in the LORD with all your heart and lean not on your own understanding; in all your ways submit to him, and he will make your paths straight."

A DIFFERENT LIFE

When I began to have clarity—to have a 3-D vision, my life took a different path. It was not the fairy tale I had envisioned, but it was something worth fighting for, worth having, worth pursuing. The things I once valued I no longer held on to with such admiration and need—the home I lived in, the clothes I wore, our status, or the company I kept. I came to the place of complete surrender. None of the material things in my life mattered, nor did people's opinion of me. Jeff and our circumstance no longer had the significance they once had. Initially, I struggled with what others thought. I worried people were talking behind our backs, wondering why we sold our house, why my husband left his practice, and why he was no longer delivering babies.

I was in a whirlwind of trying to survive this crisis and attempting to define a new normal. The only thing that would steady the storm was God's truth. I had to cleanse my filter by reading the Bible and understanding God was in control, not Jeff's addiction. God's Word removed fear—the fear of being left alone to raise our children by myself, the fear of being judged by other people, the fear of not having the provision to survive if my husband were to relapse, the fear of not being good enough. These fears no longer consumed me. I was not afraid, but I was filled with hope, courage, and strength. I believed God had a bigger plan, and I understood he was in control. Because I trusted in God, I let him become my anchor. I came to the place where I could let go of all the things I thought were important, necessary, and valuable. I surrendered my heart—the emotions that determined my choices, including my greatest fears.

Deciding to trust in God's nature and character helped me change my perception of my circumstance. I realized God was my healer, my provider, and my redeemer. Realizing he was for me and not against me gave me a new perspective. I realized if I lost everything but still had Christ, I could get through anything, but losing my faith and connection with Christ would be devastating because I would not have a purpose without him. I would give up and lose hope. With this new perspective, I was able to let God rebuild our lives and restore our brokenness.

We moved out of the city into a small town where we bought a one-hundred-year-old historic house that needed a great deal of work. I never dreamed I would end up in a rural part of Texas living in an old house with creaky floors and more DIY projects than I could ever manage, but I was happy. Happy because my husband was clean of any drugs, my children were able to run around and enjoy a different kind of life than I had ever known, and I was watching God restore the things I felt I had lost early on in this journey. He was restoring trust in our marriage and building hope in a new future. Jeff and I opened a small OB/GYN office that was thriving. It was growing into a community outreach for underserved pregnant women in the community—a much-needed service. Spiritually our lives were growing deeper in relationship with Christ and with each other. Yes, the journey was challenging, but it was also beautiful. Our new life was hard, but it was also easy. It was raw, but it was also gentle. It was an adventure for sure. I can say with absolute certainty that I could not have walked this path without Christ by my side. He was my anchor; he steadied my ship and calmed the seas every time there was a surge in the waves.

Understanding the power of your perceptions will strengthen your ability to see beyond your circumstance. Seeing past your pain is much easier when you have faith. Understanding the nature of God and who he is will cleanse your mental filter. Measuring your experiences against the truth of God's Word can change the perception of what you see sitting right in front of you!

HELPFUL TOOLS

1. What perceptions do you think you have that become like evidence in a trial—evidence that supports or reinforces your beliefs about yourself, God, and others? Record your thoughts in your journal.

2. Ask yourself how clean or dirty the window is that you use to look out and view your life circumstances. Write down any thoughts or ideas that you think may be tainting your view of reality.

3. Draw a picture of a funnel that you think represents your mental filter. Write words inside the funnel that describe your beliefs. For example, you can write words like *shame, doubt, fear, anxiety, unlucky, power, prestige, control, guarantee, hope, peace, faith, assurance,* or *confidence.* Come up with your own words. Be more specific, or even creative. There is no right or wrong response.

4. If you find you have written some words you think can taint the truth, draw another filter with new words you think are more representative of the truth.

5. Place both filters side by side and write down how these words impact your perception of your circumstances.

6. Look for Scripture passages that either support the words you have written as truth or expose them as lies.

4
A Cup of Shame
Breaking Through Strongholds

Sitting on a wooden pew in the front row, I was too young to understand the emotions flooding over me. Shame, guilt, sadness, and regret engulfed my mind, my heart, and my little body. But mostly, I felt relieved.

It was my grandfather's funeral. I was twelve.

I grew up in a conservative home where I learned sin would keep me out of heaven. My Sunday school teacher taught me sin required immediate forgiveness. Going down to the altar to repent at the end of a service was customary in my church. Most individuals sitting in the congregation accepted the pastor's invitation to rise from their seats, walk to the front of the church, and kneel at the foot of the altar, asking God to forgive them. Repentance occurred not once, but over and over and over again; it was a weekly ritual for most people, including me. Sunday after Sunday, I learned I could lose my salvation because of unforgiven sin. I lived in constant fear of making a mistake, falling into sin, or failing God without getting a chance to ask him to forgive me.

The practice of repenting and recommitting my heart to God each Sunday supposedly assured God would allow me into heaven. But a secret lurked in the shadows of my heart. I believed this secret could not be forgiven. Though I said, "I'm sorry, God" repeatedly, I still feared he would cast me aside.

As a child, I served God not only out of fear but out of love. I saw goodness in him. I went to Sunday school, children's church, and camp, where I learned of his love and mercy. We sang songs that made me happy inside. I was taught Bible stories about miracles that gave me hope. Though I longed for happiness and wanted comfort, these experiences eluded me. I wanted to be one of those little children I saw in picture books, climbing into Jesus' lap, welcoming the touch of his loving embrace. I longed to be normal like they appeared to be when they sat at his feet while he told them a captivating story. I craved their innocence, purity, and happiness. I wanted to feel Jesus' arms tight around me, keeping me safe and shielding me from the world—from everything.

Especially my grandfather. My life was far different from the idyllic scene I saw in picture books. I hid a shameful secret, dragging it behind me like a stack of timbered wood. Each time I saw my grandfather, I knew his intention. The reality of his mission filled me with dread and anguish.

During my youngest years of life, I carried an enormous amount of guilt and shame. Though I repented over and over, week after week, I still felt unforgiven. Weighed down by burdens children are not designed to carry, I wanted to relieve the guilt. Release the shame. Stop the trauma. But I didn't know how.

When my mom got the call that my grandfather had a heart attack, we rushed to the hospital. Along the way, I asked her if we could pray with him when we arrived in his room. I wondered out loud if we could get him to ask Jesus to forgive him of his sins. She agreed that talking to him and asking him to pray was a good idea.

I sat next to her in the car, thinking if I could get him to repent, God would forgive him for his sin. Relieved by his possible salvation, I thought, *At least I will not be responsible for him not getting to go to heaven.* She drove fast. When we arrived, we rushed to his hospital room. But we got there too late. He was dead. I went numb. Years later, I would learn, with my grandfather's last breaths, he had asked to see me. But that was never to be.

On the day we rushed to the hospital, all I knew was I hadn't made it there in time. I had no idea he had asked to see me. There are times when I wonder what would have happened if I had gotten the chance to talk to him that day.

That Saturday afternoon at the funeral, in that tiny church, I wanted to run away because of the sinister secret. The crushing weight from concealing this ugly truth pushed down on my frail, twelve-year-old body. I felt broken and damaged. *I should have done something,* I told myself. The thoughts pounded in my head. *I should have stopped him and told him it was wrong! I should have told him about Jesus. Now it's too late! It's my fault he's in hell.*

I broke down crying—a heaving, inconsolable cry. I'm sure everyone thought I was devastated because my grandfather had died. I was devastated, but not because he had passed away. His fate, I believed, was my doing, and the burden of his eternal destination was too much for me to bear. My heart did not ache for his passing. I actually felt relieved, as if I had turned the final page in this chapter. His death meant he wouldn't, couldn't hurt me anymore.

Beginning when I was three or four, he threatened me: "If you tell your mother our secret, I will never be allowed to see either of you again." He made it clear if I told anyone, it would be my fault.

So, I remained silent.

Haunted by what I believed was his permanent resting place, I left the funeral that day harboring the nearly decade-old secret accompanied with a lifetime of shame. I thought I was dirty, flawed, and damaged as a person, leaving me with the core belief, "I am damaged goods. I am unworthy of love." As a child, how could I know these core beliefs would grow into malignant roots taking hold of my thoughts, feelings, emotions, and behaviors? This unwelcome tragedy left me with the wreckage of emotional turmoil and its aftermath of shame, intrusively showing up when I least expected it.

SHAME

Shame is a powerful emotion that leaves you feeling like something is wrong with you. It is a learned response created from experiences that generate thoughts of self-consciousness, inadequacy, and unworthiness. Because children are more vulnerable than adults, shame typically begins early in childhood. Children encounter experiences and absorb words on a daily basis that they unknowingly allow to influence their well-being. Because children do not know how to dispute shame, it quickly takes root in their minds. Shame does not always result from abuse. It can happen on the playground if a peer makes a thoughtless remark. Shame can creep its way into any child's life, inadvertently planting itself into his or her belief system. When fully formed, these roots develop into core beliefs, such as: "There is something wrong with me," "I am damaged goods," "I don't measure up," "I am worthless," "I am unlovable," and so on.

Children whose worth is not validated by those closest to them believe this lack of acceptance makes them unlovable and worthless. These feelings create deep-seated beliefs: "I am damaged. I don't deserve love." These thoughts and feelings follow them into adulthood, shaping their self-esteem and dictating their behavior. For instance, they may mask feelings of inadequacy and unworthiness as adults by sabotaging relationships. They can become untrustworthy, unreliable, aloof, or controlling. Their beliefs of shame are then reinforced when the relationship fails, proving to themselves they were right all along—*I am damaged.*

The emotional response of shame gains momentum when circumstances seem to spotlight your personal flaws and insecurities. After a humiliating experience, an internal dialogue develops: *I always do stupid things, I hate myself.* These thoughts attempt to confirm the shameful beliefs occurring in your mind, leaving you feeling defective, broken, and damaged.

You may be experiencing shame that is so deep you believe you are beyond repair. This overwhelming sense of shame can take over your rational thinking, affecting your decisions and choices. For example, a recent divorce or the loss of a friendship leads you to believe you are defective and unworthy of love. As a result, you tell yourself, *I am not good enough; I am a failure; I am worthless.* Consequently, you feel unlovable, inferior, and damaged. As a result, you isolate and refuse to engage in meaningful relationships. This manner of thinking, feeling, and reacting turns into a vicious cycle.

The shame cycle looks like this:

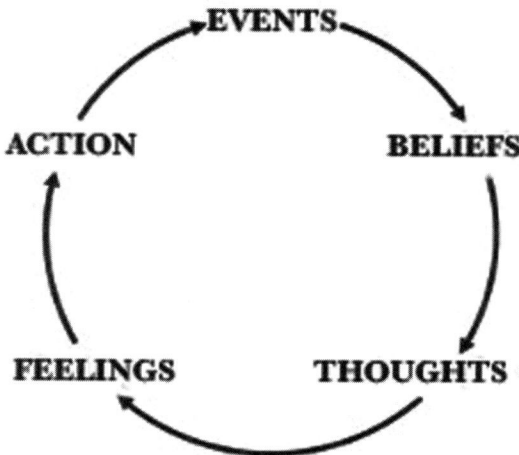

EVENTS

ACTION

BELIEFS

FEELINGS

THOUGHTS

Event: First you experience an event, such as divorce or loss of friendship.

Beliefs: Then you have a subconscious core belief: *I am defective and unworthy of love.*

Thoughts: Next, you begin thinking, *I am not good enough. I am a failure. I am worthless.*

Feelings: These thoughts cause you to feel unlovable, inferior, and damaged.

Actions: Your feelings then motivate your behavior: isolation and disengagement.

New Event: Because of this cycle of beliefs, thoughts, feelings, and behaviors, you have a new event—having no meaningful relationships. You are lonely.

This cycle often repeats itself, working like this: behaviors of isolation cause a lack of intimacy in relationships→confirming your belief you are unworthy of love→you begin thinking again, *I am not good enough*→which leads you to feel lonely, depressed, and hopeless→and you continue to isolate and withdraw from others, and the cycle continues.

CHALLENGING THE CYCLE

In my experience as a therapist, I have come to believe that to successfully stop the cycle of shame, you have to apply both the Word of God and proven cognitive-behavioral strategies. The cycle of shame will continue to repeat itself until you challenge and replace your core beliefs and thoughts. Stopping the cycle requires you to see your circumstances from a biblical and unbiased perspective. Knowing what the Bible says about who you are as a believer and understanding the facts of your situation will help you separate truth from lies.

For example, you lose your job because of company layoffs→which triggers your core belief "I am not good enough"→you tell yourself you are a failure→you feel incompetent→you don't believe you can get a new, even better job. With you being either jobless or in a position for which you are overqualified, your thoughts and feelings of inadequacy continue.

Challenging the facts will help you draw out the lie. First, look at what the Bible says about who you are. Scripture tells you: God created you in his image (Genesis 1:27). You are his workmanship (Ephesians 2:10). These passages from the Bible let you know your value comes from God, not from your job. And yes, you may be unemployed, but not because you failed to measure up as an employee. Your employers did not make this decision based on your incompetence. It was simply an economic decision. Knowing these truths in the context of your circumstance and the Word of God exposes the lie that you are not good enough.

To uproot your faulty core beliefs buried in shame, you have to

1. step back,
2. acknowledge the facts,
3. reject the lie, and
4. replace it with truth.

SHAME VERSUS GUILT

Many individuals use "guilt" and "shame" interchangeably, but they are extremely different. Shame is a deep-seated core belief, describing who you believe you are. Guilt, on the other hand, is a description of your mistake. Simply put, shame says: "I am a mistake." Guilt says: "I made a mistake."

Guilt is the conscious realization that you have done something wrong. It is a healthy indicator that lets you know you have made a mistake. It's a feeling of regret. To relieve yourself from feeling guilt in a healthy and appropriate manner, you can either correct your wrongdoing or, in the case that you have transgressed against another individual, make amends to the person you have hurt.

Feeling guilty after making a mistake is a reasonable, oftentimes constructive response, but if left unchecked, shame can creep in and ultimately act as a harmful force on your self-image. While guilt allows for reconciliation without negatively shaping the essence of who you are, shame pushes you into defining yourself by your mistakes.

When crippled by shame, you may find it difficult—even impossible—to feel guilt without feeling shame. Whenever you make a mistake, you tell yourself you not only *messed up*, but *you are messed up*. Or *I did not just make a mistake; I am a mistake*. Shameful thoughts such as these take control of your ability to distinguish between guilt and shame. The two intertwine. When this happens, you begin to believe that each and every one of your mistakes reflects who you are.

In order to actually feel better after making a mistake, you must oppose the urge to absorb shame. Remaining in a state of shame will not allow you to feel any differently after correcting your wrongdoing. However, once you are able to successfully embrace feelings of guilt without the presence of shame, you are able to move on free from the constraints that shame puts on your sense of self. Unfortunately, this is easier said than done. If you find yourself trapped in a cycle of shame, you may believe the only way to relieve the feelings of self-worthlessness is to mask your shame in order to hide your imperfections and prevent yourself from feeling vulnerable.

MASKING SHAME

When overcome by shame and insecurity, you fear your imperfections will be exposed to others, and you will likely attempt to mask these feelings. Having your faults displayed for all to see whenever you make a mistake intensifies your feelings of shame. It leaves you feeling exposed, like standing naked in the middle of a crowd immediately wanting to cover up! Covering shame is a defense mechanism used to convince yourself and others you are not damaged.

When my youngest daughter, Maddie, was in sixth grade, she came face-to-face with the power of shame. She learned shame could dictate a person's intrapersonal beliefs about themselves impacting their actions toward others. One of her closest friends, whom she had known since the second grade, was rude to her at school. She came home one afternoon, crying. When I asked her what was wrong, she told me one of her best friends, Carla, would not let her sit with her at lunch. Maddie explained a new, pretty girl had entered her class at the beginning of the year. According to Maddie, everyone liked this new girl and wanted to be her friend. At lunch, it appeared only certain people were allowed to sit at the new girl's table. On this particular day, Maddie noticed Carla had a seat at this "special" table, so Maddie asked Carla if she could sit there, but Carla said no. Having experienced this rejection, Maddie got her feelings hurt and walked away.

As Maddie tearfully shared her experience with me, I said to her, "Carla's rejection, I believe, has nothing to do with you."

Perplexed, Maddie replied, "What do you mean?"

I explained, "This behavior is most likely about her shame. She probably feels bad and insecure about herself and thinks she has to have certain people around her to feel accepted. She knows you like her, but she is uncertain what others think. Having you as a friend, in her mind, does not elevate her social status. Carla feels inferior. She thinks acceptance from the popular crowd will make those feelings go away."

Although this is an example of typical adolescent behavior, it demonstrates how shame can dictate feelings and actions. Trying to hide her shame, Carla acted like someone she wasn't. Ordinarily kind and sweet, she became rude and inconsiderate to Maddie despite their deep friendship. These characteristics were not typical for Carla. Feelings of insecurity took over her behavior. By surrounding herself with popular kids, Carla felt important and valuable, but this decision led her to reject Maddie.

Shame can lead you to act in ways you would not ordinarily behave. When you feel inferior and exposed, your immediate reaction is to hide or cover up like Carla. I believe Carla felt insecure and feared rejection by the popular crowd. To cover up her insecurities, she pretended she was better than Maddie. Declining Maddie's request to sit with her that day at lunch made her feel important and in control.

When Carla rejected her, Maddie immediately blamed herself and began to think, *I am not good enough; I don't measure up; I'm not important.*

Maddie didn't realize Carla's actions had more to do with Carla's feelings of shame than with Maddie's value. When I pointed this out, Maddie realized how shame can influence and even dictate someone's actions. As her mom, I could see shame was beginning to surface, and I didn't want it to take deeper root in Maddie's mind—because taking root is what shame does.

When individuals feel damaged or devalued, they conclude there must be something wrong with them. Behaviors have the ability to expose core beliefs rooted in shame. Your insecure feelings will motivate you to hide your shame through your behavior. There are several ways to cover up or mask shame. You can blame others, placate others, condemn others, or confuse others.

Blaming Others: Blamers always find fault and never fully accept responsibility for their actions. They believe that if they can find an excuse for their behavior, their imperfections will not be exposed.

Placating Others: Individuals who placate always want to please others even when pleasing comes with personal cost. They typically look for the approval of others and avoid conflict whenever possible. They believe having this approval will cover any weaknesses or deficiencies.

Condemning Others: Condemners are arrogant. They always have answers and are overly critical of others. They believe if they are better or smarter, they will not be inferior to others.

Confusing Others: Being aloof sends mixed messages to people. They do not reveal how they are feeling. They believe keeping individuals at a distance protects anyone from seeing their faults.

Covering up shame is a method for coping but often comes with a price. It may cost intimacy, vulnerability, authenticity, and even relationships altogether. Acknowledging the lies existing within your shame will help you avoid masking your feelings. Knowing the truth about the core of who you are is the best defense. God's Word contains the truth. When Christ died on the cross, your sins—all of them—were forgiven. You are redeemed. Through salvation and redemption, Christ now defines your value and worth, not your mistakes.

Second Corinthians 5:17 says, "Therefore if any man be in Christ, he is a new creature: old things are passed away; behold, all things are become new" (KJV). Christ has made you into a new person regardless of your past experiences. Being made into a new creation is not conditional. This rebirth is for everyone who accepts Christ as their Savior.

TWO WEDDINGS

In the book of Genesis, a powerful story comes to life of two Hebrew women who stood face-to-face with their own demons of self-defeating lies and crippling insecurities. These embedded lies ensnared sisters Leah and Rachel into a web of shame, leaving them in sad and depressing circumstances as they struggled to find their way out of despair. Leah, in my opinion, believed she would never be good enough. Rachel, I believe, felt she could not live up to her husband's expectations. Pity, self-doubt, and fear took root in both of them.

Rachel's beauty had stolen the heart of Jacob, a hardworking man committed to obtaining the woman of his dreams. Jacob loved Rachel and wanted to marry her, but he had to receive the blessing of her father, Laban. Laban gave him permission to marry Rachel in exchange for seven years of laboring in his fields. Rachel's captivating beauty and Jacob's love for her secured his decision to enter into a seven-year contract working in Laban's fields in order to receive Rachel's hand in marriage.

After seven long years of labor and hard work, the wedding day finally arrived. I can only imagine the excitement Jacob felt. He had faithfully worked day after day, knowing Rachel would soon be his prize. When the day approached, he must have been overcome with joy, but something unexpected and unimaginable hid just beneath the surface.

Waking up the next morning, Jacob eagerly anticipated his new life with Rachel, but a nightmare he had never anticipated unfolded in its place. The morning after the wedding, a beautiful sunrise most likely woke Jacob from his sleep. Leaning over to kiss his new wife, whose face must have been hidden from him the night before, he felt excited and overjoyed to see her for the first time as his wife. But he looked into her face and realized he had not married the love of his life—he had married her sister Leah.

Infuriated, Jacob stormed out of the marriage tent to confront Laban, abandoning Leah and leaving her feeling dismissed and rejected. Alone with her thoughts, the lies must have taunted her: *"You are damaged, you are not good enough, you are a mistake, you are unlovable, ugly, hideous . . ."* She spiraled into her shame, deeper than ever before.

When Jacob confronted Laban, Laban excused himself by citing a local custom that a younger daughter could not marry ahead of an older one. Then Laban insisted Jacob work another seven years but allowed him to immediately take Rachel as his bride. Jacob kept Leah as his wife but was never in love with her.

I cannot imagine how humiliating this must have been for Leah. Knowing her marriage originated in deceit and manipulation must have made her feel worthless and used. I can envision her plummeting into the depths of shame from believing she had no other choice but to accept the idea of being second to her sister, a burden, an afterthought.

When Leah was alone, she must have experienced moments where she dreamed of Jacob taking her into his loving arms while whispering into her ear, "You are beautiful." But her thoughts were interrupted by the nagging lie, *I am not worthy of love and affection.*

Disheartened and deeply wounded, Leah found herself in an indifferent and calloused world. Bearing children became the one thing that gave her purpose in the shadow of her shame. Revealing her true feelings when she gave birth to her first son, she said, "It is because the LORD has seen my misery. Surely my husband will love me now" (Genesis 29:32). Defeated again by her shame, she said at the birth of her second son, "Because the LORD has heard that I am hated, he has given me this son also" (v. 33 ESV). She named him Simeon, which means God Has Heard.

Desperately wanting to be loved but thinking she never would be, Leah gave up hope that she would ever be good enough. At her core, I imagine, she convinced herself she was unlovable. These beliefs, thoughts, and feelings affected her actions as a wife, mother, and sister.

Rachel also experienced core beliefs rooted in shame. Although beautiful and adored by Jacob, she remained barren for many years. Because she could not have children, she, like her sister, felt damaged. I imagine she told herself she did not deserve Jacob's love. Haunted by the fear of losing his loyalty and adoration because she was childless, these thoughts caused her to feel threatened by her sister's fertility. At her core she believed she was inferior and feared Jacob would abandon her and withdraw his love. Just like her sister, these core beliefs were rooted in shame, creating a fortress in Rachel's mind, and tainting her perception of herself. Both women were driven by feelings of shame. Their minds were polluted by false beliefs, causing bitterness and animosity to exist within their household.

Leah struggled with finding her place. Having shame already deeply planted in her mind, the circumstance of her marriage fit directly into her own narrative that she was not good enough. I imagine she placated as an attempt to cover her shame. She believed having the ability to bear children would shine favor on her, but her self-loathing thoughts of being unlovable eluded the favor she had hoped to receive. Seeing

Jacob look into the eyes of Rachel became the evidence Leah needed to support her feelings of shame.

I would guess Rachel would have condemned Leah by punishing her with words. I believe Rachel felt threatened by Leah's fertility. Her inability to bear children fueled her thoughts of shame. Like her sister, she probably believed the same lie, "I am not good enough." You can see the irony. Though the details of their circumstances were different, their thoughts and beliefs—*I am damaged and unworthy of love*—were likely the same. They despised each other for different reasons. The animosity in both of them was embedded in the same web of shame-induced lies.

The underlying beliefs of shame are not unique. Circumstances may vary but core beliefs remain the same: "I am not good enough, I am unlovable, I am damaged," and so on. These beliefs bury themselves deep within the mind, creating strongholds that are difficult to destroy.

Maybe you are like Leah and have woken up in complete shock at your circumstance, thinking to yourself, *How did I end up here?* You realize your life has suddenly changed forever and you are wondering how you are going to survive. Maybe you are like Rachel: you believe your inability to perform robs you of your value and worth. Before you know it, shame has taken root in your mind and in your heart. You blame yourself. Your heavy-hearted and hopeless feelings become overwhelming. You have a stronghold of shame that feels insurmountable.

RECOGNIZING STRONGHOLDS

A stronghold is a belief, a lie, an assumption that builds a fortress around your mind tainting your perception of reality. Strongholds keep you from changing your core beliefs. This is why you cannot easily change the way you think. Most often, when you find yourself stuck in a pattern of thoughts, feelings, and behaviors, it is because of a strong-hold. For example, my stronghold of shame was so deep I believed with absolute certainty I was damaged. This belief kept me from experiencing the redemptive power of Christ in my life. I did not believe what the Bible said about salvation, making me a new person. I thought my offenses disqualified my ability to be fully cleansed. This belief affected my actions and choices.

Shameful thoughts burrowed deeply into my mind, reinforcing the lie that told me I had no worth. My feelings of shame caused me to settle for less, to give up on my education, and to compromise my values.

I had teachers who tried to encourage me to think and expect more of myself, but I did not listen. I would think, *Why try? I am not smart enough to succeed. People don't like me. I am better off staying in the background. Something is wrong with me. Best not rock the boat.* These thoughts stood in the way of my desire to work hard. I believed I was inferior and incapable. I felt inadequate, incompetent, and useless, so I gave up trying to succeed. It seemed pointless. These self-defeating thoughts and feelings of shame became a cycle that crippled my self-esteem.

As a young woman, I thought furthering my education was out of the question, but my mother believed differently. She insisted I enroll in college. The fall semester after I graduated from high school, I registered as a freshman at a Bible college near my home. As expected, I did not do well. It was not until my junior year that I realized for the first time that I could succeed if I worked hard enough.

A professor in the psychology department called me out of class one day and asked to meet with me. Nervously, I sat in his office wondering what he could possibly have to say to me. I thought, *Why did he call me here? Am I such a bad student he is going to tell me to drop out of school? Maybe he is going to tell me I am better off doing something else. Is he going to ask what I think is wrong with me? I can't do this; I want to leave* . . . These thoughts flooded my mind, rapidly increasing my anxiety. Buried deep in my mind was a stronghold, my core belief: *I am damaged.* I felt like I did not belong. I wanted to take off running. I wanted to run away from the immense amount of shame hovering over me as I sat quietly waiting for him in the stillness of his empty office.

Earlier in the semester, he gave our class an assignment to write a paper describing our childhood. I was terrified. I thought, *What am I going to write? Should I make something up and write what I wished my childhood had been like, or should I tell the horrible truth?* I struggled for days, wondering what I should do. I finally decided to tell the truth. Writing the paper was torture. I felt ashamed, exposed, embarrassed, and mortified about what he would think of me. Sitting in his office, I felt sick to my stomach, thinking I should have never written that paper.

He walked in, sat directly across from me, and pointedly asked, "Do you think your childhood experiences have something to do with your poor performance at school?"

"No . . .," I murmured. I was ashamed even talking about how badly I was doing. "I'm not very smart," I shrugged.

"That's a lie," he said without apology for the bluntness. "I believe you are one of my smartest students."

I sat in disbelief, feeling dumbfounded. I thought he was crazy.

He continued. "Because of the trauma you suffered as a child, you don't do well in school. You believe you are broken and inferior." He kept pushing. "As a result of this belief, you don't try. You don't participate in class, and you fail to study. This is why you don't do well—it has nothing to do with how smart you are."

We both sat in silence. His words hung over me as though there was nowhere for them to go. I wanted desperately to grab every word and hold on to them and pull them in close. I wanted to trust he was speaking the truth, but what he claimed notably contradicted everything I believed.

Over the course of that semester, he helped me identify the beliefs in my mind holding me hostage to shame. I also learned how much power a stronghold can have in one's life. He showed me how to identify the lies and tear down the stronghold of shame. As I began to see my worth and value slowly emerge, I diligently applied myself. I became a straight-A student and went on to get my master's degree—something I had never dreamed would be possible.

Strongholds build a fortress around your mind and block the truth from entering. This is why simply trying to make yourself think differently doesn't work. You try your best to think more positively, only to be hijacked by your feelings of shame. These feelings convince you to believe the lie. This process becomes a vicious pattern of beliefs, thoughts, feelings, and actions.

Beliefs→Thoughts→Feelings→Actions

FINDING MORE EVIDENCE

Finding evidence to support the lies that come from shame is how strongholds gain momentum to move past your thoughts and into your core belief system. Whenever you think you have found proof of your shame, your lies are reinforced.

Event→You make a mistake

Core Belief→you believe you are not good enough

Thoughts→you think you're a failure

Feelings→you feel depressed

Behavior→you stop trying

Core Belief→you believe more strongly you are not good enough

Thoughts→you continue to think you are a failure

Feelings→you feel more depressed

Behavior→you give up.

Your lack of positive experiences from refusing to try reinforces your thoughts of being a failure. This becomes your pattern.

The more evidence you think you find, the stronger your core beliefs become. Evidence makes a stronghold grow a taller and more powerful fortress of shame in your mind. Take, for example, Leah and Rachel. Rachel used her infertility as evidence she was not good enough, and Leah thought Jacob's rejection supported the belief she was unlovable. These lies became a stronghold in their minds, creating an impenetrable fortress and destroying their ability to accept the truth about who they were. Shame dictated their feelings and behaviors.

As a young woman, I found evidence to support the lies rooted in my own shame. Lies that said, *I am damaged, inferior, and tarnished.* I found proof whenever I made a mistake, received poor grades, or had a failed relationship. Since I believed I was not good enough, I gave up trying. I used my failures as evidence to support my core beliefs.

REMOVING STRONGHOLDS

Feelings of shame are deeply buried within a false core belief system in desperate need of uprooting. Core beliefs dig themselves deep into your mind making it difficult to pull them out, keeping you ensnared in your shame. A stronghold has to be broken by something greater than yourself. Think of a stronghold like a corkscrew. A cork nestled tightly into a bottle is impossible to remove. A corkscrew is designed to twist into the cork. Once it is nestled in, the grip is tight enough to pull the cork out of the bottle. When it comes out, the corkscrew remains in the cork. It is impossible to pull the corkscrew out without deliberately twisting it. A stronghold works the same way. It twists itself deeply into your mind by gripping tightly to your belief system and distorting the truth about who you are. This makes it difficult to eliminate false beliefs.

Because a stronghold is twisted tight into your heart and mind, removing it is not an exercise that happens in one fell swoop. It is a process requiring discipline and hard work. Like a corkscrew that cannot be pulled directly out of the cork, neither can a stronghold be instantly removed. It has to be a careful and methodical untwisting of a deep belief rooted in your mind. When the lies have become so profoundly embedded into your mind, they produce automatic emotional responses, and you instantly react before you have a chance to change your thinking. Your reaction to the situation originates from a position of shame, leaving you with the aftermath of your actions.

Enlisting the help of a counselor is often essential to overcoming your faulty core beliefs. When I first learned the power shame had in my life as a college student, I did not have the skill or biblical knowledge to eliminate all of the lies entangled in my mind. My journey to fully release the strongholds in my mind required professional counseling and spiritual mentoring from a seasoned believer in my local church.

Along with the support of others, overcoming a stronghold requires enlisting the supernatural power of Christ to give you the strength and mental ability you will need to persevere in demolishing your core beliefs. God will give you the insight and strength to help you dispute and eliminate the lies by employing his truth. Using the Bible as your weapon will give you the knowledge and power to overcome the lies that are holding you captive.

As a Christian, you have the ability to access a power source greater than yourself. After Christ died, resurrected, and ascended to heaven, the Holy Spirit came to live within all Christians. Peter confirmed this when he said to the believers, "Repent and be baptized every one of you in the name of Jesus Christ for the forgiveness of your sins, and you will receive the gift of the Holy Spirit" (Acts 2:38 ESV).

The Bible tells us the Holy Spirit is our teacher, comforter, intercessor, counselor, helper, and source of power:

- **Teacher:** "But the Helper, the Holy Spirit, whom the Father will send in my name, he will teach you all things and bring to your remembrance all that I have said to you" (John 14:26 ESV).

- **Comforter:** "More than that, we rejoice in our sufferings, knowing that suffering produces endurance, and endurance produces character, and character produces hope, and hope does not put us to shame, because God's love has been poured into our hearts through the Holy Spirit who has been given to us" (Romans 5:3–5).

- **Intercessor:** "Likewise the Spirit helps us in our weakness. For we do not know what to pray for as we ought, but the Spirit himself intercedes for us with groanings too deep for words" (Romans 8:26 ESV).

- **Counselor:** "And the Spirit of the LORD shall rest upon him, the Spirit of wisdom and understanding, the Spirit of counsel and might, the Spirit of knowledge and the fear of the LORD" (Isaiah 11:2 ESV).

- **Helper:** "And I will ask the Father, and he will give you another Helper, to be with you forever, even the Spirit of truth, whom the world cannot receive, because it neither sees him nor knows him. You know him, for he dwells with you and will be in you" (John 14:16–17 ESV).

- **Source of Power:** "May the God of hope fill you with all joy and peace in believing, so that by the power of the Holy Spirit you may abound in hope" (Romans 15:13 ESV).

The Holy Spirit will help you identify your false core beliefs by showing you the truth in God's Word. You can use this truth to replace the lies embedded in your mind. Understanding the power you have through the Holy Spirit gives you the supernatural ability to demolish strongholds. Paul wrote in 2 Corinthians 10:5, "We destroy arguments and every lofty opinion raised against the knowledge of God, and take every thought captive to obey Christ" (ESV).

While this passage is speaking truth and is necessary for you to understand the power of your thoughts, it is often oversimplified. When you read the phrase "Take your thoughts captive," you may imagine this means to imprison your thoughts and put them behind bars, but this is not exactly what it means to take your thoughts captive. Yes, you have to eliminate the ensnaring lies, but removing these lies takes time and effort. When you simply make the decision to remove your thoughts, they don't go away automatically.

Think of a criminal who needs to be apprehended and put behind bars. Before you can imprison him, you have to put forth a plan and then take the time and effort required to catch him and put him under arrest. Your thoughts work in the same way. When your thoughts lie and steal your self-worth, they need to be captured and imprisoned by developing a plan of action. Like arresting a criminal, capturing your thoughts is a process that takes time and requires hard work and perseverance.

So, how do you take thoughts captive? I wish there was an easy step-by-step solution, but the truth is, this is a process that is different for every person. There are several strategies and techniques that you can employ to help you remove a stronghold of shame in your mind.

Mindfulness

Rather than fighting the thoughts in your head, let them pass by you without holding on to them. Notice the uncomfortable feelings your thoughts create without letting them dictate the way you feel about yourself and how you choose to behave. Maybe you notice the feeling of nausea or a tightening in the pit in your stomach when you have the thought, *I am stupid.* Don't let that distressing feeling cause you to act badly by isolating or curling up in a ball and avoiding certain people or things. Instead, be aware that your thoughts are just thoughts. They do not define you; you are not your thoughts.

Be mindful of your inner self and label thoughts as thoughts and feelings as feelings because they don't have to be anything more than that. Just because you have the thought, *I am not good enough,* does not mean you have to believe it. It simply came into your mind for a reason you may not know yet, and that is okay. You can let it come and go into your mind without attachment or judgment of the thought. Identify the precipitating event and acknowledge your thoughts are valid even if they are negative. Everything has a cause, and so do your thoughts. You are not a bad person for thinking bad thoughts. Just let your thoughts pass through your mind like leaves on a stream, boats in a lake, or birds in the sky, and keep doing the next thing without letting your thoughts take root and have power over you.

Thought Stopping

Imagine a stop sign whenever you have a thought that reinforces your feelings of shame. The purpose of seeing a stop sign in your mind is to allow you the time to pause and interrupt the pattern of negative thinking so you can dispute it. This can be done by quoting verses in the Bible or reciting positive affirmations about yourself. Let's say you have the thought, *I hate myself,* and you start cycling through your pattern of behavior. Imagine a stop sign, big and red, before you begin to spiral and let the thought have power over you. Now, begin to tell yourself affirmations such as, "I am loved, valued, and worthy of affection." Recite a verse to yourself that reinforces these truths or recite another verse that comforts you, like "I am fearfully and wonderfully made" (Psalm 139:14). I have had clients who have placed Post-it Notes on their mirror or on the dashboard of their car to help remind them of the truth of who they are.

Prayer and Meditation

Pray and ask God to remove the shameful thought and replace it with the truth. There are several ways you can pray. I have found praising and worshiping God through music and speaking out loud the beauty and attributes of God is a great way to begin. After spending some time worshiping, you can pray prayers of confession and petition. When praying in this manner, you simply ask God for what you need. I personally pray as if I am having a conversation with God. I confess my sin, and I ask him to forgive me. Then I tell him what I am feeling and thinking, and I ask him to help me, comfort me, and guide me. When I am struggling to overcome a stronghold, I pray prayers of warfare.

Your mind is often a battlefield where Satan tries to defeat you by filling it with lies. He likes to distort and taint the truth. This is when you, as a believer, can take authority over Satan by praying in the name of Jesus. Paul wrote in 2 Corinthians 10:4, "For the weapons of our warfare are not carnal, but mighty through God to the pulling down of strongholds" (KJV). He also explained in Philippians 2:9–11, "Therefore God has highly exalted him and bestowed on him the name that is above every name, so that at the name of Jesus every knee should bow, in heaven and on earth and under the earth, and every tongue confess that Jesus Christ is Lord, to the glory of God the Father" (ESV). End your time in prayer with prayers of thanksgiving, thanking God for what he has done and is going to do in your life. In Philippians 4:6, Paul wrote, "Do not be anxious about anything, but in everything by prayer and supplication with thanksgiving let your requests be made known to God" (ESV). Throughout your day, meditate on the truth of who God is and what he has said in his Word.

Bible Study

Studying the Bible is the best way to know what the truth actually is. There are many different Bible studies you can choose to assist you in learning Scripture. Find one that best suits your style of learning. Write down and memorize scriptures. When your mind drifts back to the lies Satan wants you to believe, remind yourself of the verses you have committed to memory.

Journaling

Journaling is a great way to keep track of your thoughts. Writing down your thoughts and feelings can often help you see a pattern. You can determine your triggering event to negative patterns in your thinking and then trace these thoughts to a core belief. You can also dispute your false core beliefs and negative thoughts as you reflect and journal about your day.

Imagery

Taking time to relax your brain and imagine a peaceful and calm place can help you refocus your thoughts. Imagine sitting and taking in the beauty that surrounds you. Be mindful of taking slow, deep breaths in through your nose and then release your breath out of your mouth. This technique enhances your ability to think clearly and relax your mind at the same time.

IF YOU FEEL LIKE A FAILURE when you attempt to stop your negative thinking, be kind to yourself, and remind yourself your beliefs are deeply rooted and not easily removed. The deeper your roots are embedded, the more time and effort it will take to expose and remove them. You are not alone. With the help of others and through the power of the Holy Spirit working in your mind, you can demolish strongholds.

If you are in a bad or painful circumstance and want to be rescued, taken away, and given a safe place, trust God is telling you the truth when he says he has come to set the captives free. "The Spirit of the Sovereign LORD is on me, because the LORD has anointed me to proclaim good news to the poor. He has sent me to bind up the brokenhearted, to proclaim freedom for the captives and release from darkness for the prisoners" (Isaiah 61:1).

In this passage, God is talking to you. It doesn't matter what lies keep you in bondage; Christ came to bring you freedom and truth. When you find yourself in a painful circumstance, and you cannot move beyond your pain to see any hope, or you are stuck in grief or hurt from a past experience and can't move forward no matter how hard you try, look to God. In his midst, there is hope. Strongholds can be broken, and shame can be defeated. When strongholds are broken, truth always prevails.

HELPFUL TOOLS

1. Write down all of your core beliefs attached to shame. Journal about how your experiences have influenced your feelings of shame.

2. Identify your shame cycle by recording the events, beliefs, thoughts, and actions that occur in a cyclic pattern.

3. Identify which mask you use when trying to cover your shame. Write down examples of how you have used the mask in your daily circumstances and relationships.

4. Distinguish the difference between shame and guilt. Ask yourself if the two are intertwined in your life. If yes, journal your experience. Start the process of untangling the two by identifying the thoughts associated with shame that have hijacked your ability to make amends and feel better.

5. Identify and write down all the strongholds that are holding you captive spiritually.

6. Determine which methods work best in taking captive the thoughts that ensnare you into a stronghold.

7. Develop a plan of action and use it whenever negative or self-defeating thoughts begin to take over.

8. Carve out time each day to pray and meditate on God's Word.

9. Find a Christian counselor and mentor to give you deeper insight and support.

10. Be patient and kind to yourself, and always remember to give yourself grace and continue to persevere.

5

A Cup of Fear

Eliminating False Core Beliefs

WHEN LIGHTNING STRIKES

*L*ate one evening in early spring, I was home alone with my young children when a terrible storm began to blow through Austin. The local news was sending out thunderstorm warnings with the possibility of strong winds, hail, and flooding. I hated when these kinds of storms would come and Jeff, my husband, wouldn't be at home. It seemed every time a thunderstorm and a threat of a tornado made its way into Austin, he was at the hospital working and I was at home by myself with the kids. For some reason, this particular storm seemed more ominous than usual.

As I tried to get my children settled in for the evening, my son, Christopher, decided he was cold. We would commonly use a space heater in our home whenever we felt a bit chilly. To avoid an electrical overload, we had to be careful which outlet we used. Not paying attention, Christopher plugged in the heater and turned it on while my daughter Tori was in the bathroom, blow-drying her hair. Suddenly, we were without electricity. He had blown a fuse. It was up to me to restore the power by locating the breaker box and flipping the tripped switch. Sadly, I had to go outside in the backyard to find the circuit board.

Armed with a flashlight, rain boots, and an umbrella, I reluctantly made my way into the dark enduring forceful winds and heavy rain.

Once I found the box, I worked furiously to open it until I realized it was locked. My stomach sank. *Where is the key?* I thought frantically. Cold and wet, I ran back into our darkened house, desperately looking for the key with my dimly lit flashlight.

I found several keys without labels in a kitchen drawer, so I quickly grabbed all of them and went back outside into the storm. Because the wind had picked up a great deal of speed, my umbrella flipped inside out. As the rain poured onto me, I struggled to snap the umbrella back into its rightful position. Making my way back to the control panel, I fought the wind and rain while trying to hold on to my umbrella, the flashlight, and several loose keys. I was a mess. Feeling abandoned and utterly alone in the storm, I wanted to cry. I thought, *How did I get here?* There I stood fighting back my tears, desperately trying to get the panel door to open. None of the keys were working. Despite my best efforts, the control panel remained locked.

I stood there for a few seconds in the stormy weather and strong winds, feeling sorry for myself and thinking, *What now?* I decided there was nothing I could do but go inside and weather the storm in the dark.

There have been many occasions where an unexpected set of circumstances threatened to take me down. Experiencing a great deal of fear, I felt alone and ill-equipped, just as I did the night of that terrible storm.

It was the summer after Tori's freshman year of college. She had experienced a successful first year at the University of Mary Hardin-Baylor, and I was looking forward to a restful extended time with her being back at home. Tori had joined an on-campus Christian ministry called Young Life. She had signed up to go with her friends to a Young Life leadership training camp in Colorado the first week of the summer break. Later that week, Tori called to check in. I noticed she was excited about all she was getting to do and learn at this camp—more excited than I had ever heard her. After hanging up the phone, I didn't know if I should have been happy for her or worried, because something didn't seem quite right. On her drive home, she called and let me know she had been up all night unable to sleep due to her excitement. Her friends were uncomfortable with her driving, so they drove her car while encouraging her to sleep in the back seat. She called me on her cell phone, talking so fast I could barely keep up with what she was trying to say. She told me she wanted to drive and believed she had more energy than her friends and said sternly, "I am not taking a nap because I need to make sure they are driving safely!" Again, I knew things were not as they should be. I pushed these thoughts away, telling myself she was just super energized by all the things she experienced and learned at this beautiful, rustic Young Life camp. I thought, *After she gets some sleep, everything will be fine.* She arrived back home at 1:00 a.m. When she came in, she was bright-eyed and ready to talk. Not something you would expect from someone who had just ridden in a car for thirteen hours without having slept the night before. I expected her to fall into bed exhausted from her lack of sleep and the long car ride home. Little did I know that a storm of monumental proportions was brewing.

I woke up early that next morning after Tori had arrived home from camp, expecting to find her asleep in her bed, but that is not what I found. When I went to her room to check on her, she was not there. Her bed that had clearly not been slept in stared back at me with a gaze as cold as stone. An ominous feeling swept over me. Panicked, I frantically ran down the stairs to try and find her. After a few minutes of searching, I found her curled up in the back seat of her car, singing and writing in her journal. Perplexed by this odd behavior, I started an aggressive line of questioning. "What are you doing?" "Why are you in your car at 5:00 a.m.?" "Why are you not asleep?" "What has gotten into you?" "What makes you think sitting in your car in the middle of the night when you should be sleeping is okay?" I insisted she go up to her room to sleep, but sleep would evade her and me for the next several weeks.

When my husband was leaving for work that morning, she ran down the stairs to tell him all the enlightenment she had received while in Colorado. It was at that point we knew she was manic. This behavior was not your average excitement; it had far exceeded what you would consider typical enthusiasm, and it had not nearly reached its peak. It was just the beginning. After several days of not sleeping, she became increasingly aggressive. She started saying things that made no sense. She cursed and hurled insults at her dad and me. This is my child who loves God and is eager to please those around her. *How could this be happening? Where has my daughter gone?* I thought. I was fearful she was gone for good, never to return to her usual self. Life had changed in an instant. Overnight she became a loose cannon.

We had no idea how to help her. She refused to sleep, and she talked without stopping. She would yell and scream at her dad and me. She threatened to harm herself and us while insisting that she was Mary, the second mother of Jesus, married to Ezekiel, and had one billion dollars in her bank account to give away to those in need. In no uncertain terms, she let us know that we would not receive a penny of that money. This kind of talk seems ludicrous now, but it was painfully real at the time.

What started as excitement quickly turned into absolute mental, emotional, and psychotic chaos. The acceleration rate of her psychosis and mania was exponential. It was like a car spinning out of control on an icy road. All I could do was turn the wheel in the direction of the spin and hope it would soon come to a stop. It didn't end, though; she kept spinning faster and faster. I did not know how to stop it. There were moments I felt as though I was spinning with her. I could not understand how my daughter so quickly spiraled into this unknown, unpredictable, and frenzied state of mind. I sat on my porch and cried, begging God to bring her back to me. It seemed to be a futile request because she appeared to not be coming back; instead, she was moving farther and farther away from us at the speed of a runaway train.

Life quickly became unmanageable. I couldn't reason with her or talk over her incessant bizarre and insane rhetoric. Completely unsolicited, she would lash out at a moment's notice. I felt like an inexperienced lion tamer trying to get an angry lioness to go into her cage. It became apparent I could not tame the lion, even though I was a trained therapist and my husband a doctor. You would think our level of knowledge and training would be enough to equip us, but all our efforts to slow the acceleration and stop the spinning failed. It became painfully evident we could no longer keep her and ourselves safe. She was spiraling faster and faster out of control. We were now several days into this psychotic insanity and faced with a long holiday weekend with no means of seeing a psychiatrist. Our only option was to admit her into the hospital. Her dad and I both had worked in psychiatric hospitals, and the last thing we ever wanted to do was to put our own daughter into one, but she was completely out of control and beyond any kind of reason. She was in danger of harming herself and posed a threat to her dad and me. We were terrified to keep her at home, and we were terrified to admit her. We went back and forth the entire weekend. Then finally, on Monday morning—Memorial Day—we made the difficult and painful decision to admit her into a psychiatric hospital.

Initially, I believed putting her into the hospital would keep her safe and allow the doctors to give her the medication she needed to sleep and stabilize. After she was stable and had slept for a few days, I thought she would simply come back home for us to enjoy the rest of the summer together. Sadly, that was not what happened. The doctors did give her medications to help her sleep and stop the psychosis, but it took the entire summer to put an end to the mania. She remained in the hospital for ten days, and after a couple of weeks at home, the mania increased, and she started showing signs of psychosis again. One evening she ran out of the house, not wearing shoes, and ran onto our long gravel driveway onto the road threatening to run into a car. Her friend who lived nearby was visiting, and she started running after her, barefoot like Tori. When we realized what was happening, her dad, grandfather, and I dropped everything to try and chase her down as well. When we caught up to her, she had to be restrained. She was no longer rational and was completely out of control. When we managed to get back to the house, I immediately called her doctor. He wanted to readmit her. I pleaded with him not to put her back into the hospital. I asked him if we could increase her medications and give her something more substantial to help her sleep. She and I had not slept for several weeks. He finally agreed she could stay home, but if she showed more signs of psychosis and was a threat to herself or others, I would have to agree to take her directly to the hospital.

That was the moment I felt there was no hope. I felt swallowed up by this uncontrollable storm. I could not see anything beyond our pain. My life had become dark and chaotic, with no clear path to find the light again. Overcome by fear, I started believing she would never be the same, and this turbulent storm would never end. I felt as though God was a million miles away. I no longer had the strength or the energy to pray. I could only lean on my friends in Dallas and trust they would pray for me. Each day was a struggle. I had no idea what to expect in the coming days. Instead of things slowly getting better, they got worse. It appeared I would have to adjust to a new normal that did not look anything like the normal I wanted to see. I was tired and wanted to throw my hands in the air and give up, but I knew deep down God was with me even though I could not feel his presence. All I had was my faith. My circumstance looked bleak and hopeless and offered me nothing but despair. I had to believe God could see what I couldn't and trust he was working on mine and Tori's behalf.

Though Tori's acceleration into mania was quick, her journey back was slow and long. She later told me she felt as if her brain was on fire. I can't imagine what that must have been like. But from my perspective being on the outside looking in, that analogy made perfect sense. It took months for the fire in her brain to extinguish, and once the fire was out, the leftover smoke spiraled her into a deep depression. There were days I wondered which was worse, the mania or the depression. Her depression was dark. There were days she did not want to live. I feared she would harm herself when I wasn't looking. On other days she could barely get herself out of bed, but over time and with a lot of prayer and effort, the light eventually came back on, and the darkness subsided. It required all of us—her dad, the doctors, the therapist, me and, of course, herself—working diligently to find a way to vanquish the fire and drive out the smoke.

We had to be patient and listen even though her words were often hurtful and did not make sense. We had to resist trying to reason with her and learn simply to be present. As a therapist, I wanted to fix her, but I came to realize fixing her was not my job. My job was simply to be her mom—a safe place for her to express herself emotionally even when her feelings were out of range. Her psychiatrist told me to let Tori's hateful and angry words fall off me. She said, "Don't take it personally—you're the safest person in her life and will get the brunt of her overwhelming emotional reactions." I had to come to a point of radical acceptance, being in the moment, and releasing all expectations for the future.

Her recovery wasn't days or even weeks. It was month after month and year after year of intense therapy, medication, prayer, and perseverance. She fought this illness and continues to fight like a warrior. Through consistent prayer, compliance in taking her medication, and regular therapy, she has figured out how to build a life worth living despite having a chronic mental illness. God saw then what I can see now—a beautiful testimony of healing, restoration, and grace.

Staying the course, especially on the darkest days, is enough. It may not feel like enough, but it is. Your faith is the source of your strength and hope. Remaining steadfast in your faith will keep one foot moving in front of the other. There will be days when you will think you can't take another step, but you can. Even if it's only one small inch, just keep moving.

Storms of life often approach quickly without warning, making you feel like the rain will sweep you away. Like me, you may scramble to find your way out of the darkness, desperate to bring back the light that so suddenly vanished, you quickly learn you don't have the key to unlock the power source to turn the light back on. Fearing the light will never come back, you feel desperate and hopeless, but your perspective, like mine, can change when you fix your eyes upon Jesus. He will help you stay the course even when you can't see the end result.

WALKING ON WATER

The biblical story of Peter walking on water powerfully illustrates this point. Peter was part of a handful of men Jesus had asked to follow him when he began his full-time ministry here on earth. These men were known as the twelve disciples. They literally followed Jesus everywhere he went while he spread the good news of the gospel. Jesus was on a mission to fulfill the messianic Old Testament prophecies. Jesus and his disciples traveled from town to town, sometimes speaking to large crowds, performing miracles, and healing the sick. He and his disciples shared the good news and told everyone he was the Son of God.

On one such occasion, five thousand people showed up to hear Jesus speak. When Jesus realized there was no food for the people to eat, he sent his disciples out to gather what food they could find. They were only able to locate a boy who had two fish and five barley loaves of bread. The disciples told Jesus this was all the food they could find. Unalarmed, Jesus simply prayed over the food, and a miracle occurred. Those two fish and five loaves of bread fed every person, including the children. Once everyone had finished eating, Jesus asked his disciples to gather up what was left over. The disciples collected twelve baskets of uneaten food. It was a true sign something extraordinary and super-natural had taken place that day.

After having fed the five thousand people who had gathered from all around to hear him speak, Jesus needed to rest. He sent the disciples ahead of him while he stayed back to rest and pray. The disciples went on ahead and got into a fishing boat to travel to the next town. Like Jesus, they too were worn out from ministering to such a large crowd of people. They made pallets for themselves at the bottom of the boat and went to sleep. Suddenly, in the middle of the night, an unforeseen storm developed. The small fishing boat was tossed back and forth, waking the disciples from their sleep. With each crashing wave, they became more and more frightened. Terrified, all of the disciples scurried around the boat, frantically gathering whatever container they could find to toss the water out of the boat to keep from sinking.

From the shore, Jesus could see the ominous clouds moving over the middle of the lake. Turbulent weather was imminent, but Jesus was not worried. He knew this was an opportunity to show the majesty of God in the middle of a terrible storm. Jesus miraculously, in all of his glory, stepped onto the water and walked toward them.

Imagine being on a small boat in the middle of a tumultuous storm with no practical means of escape. It was dark and chaotic, with torrential rains and rushing winds most likely blinding the disciples ability to see. I would think the roar of the thunder and the forceful winds would have been so loud and boisterous that they could barely hear themselves speak. I am sure they wondered if they would have the strength, courage, and means to ride out the storm. Fear was inescapable.

Desperately attempting to get water out of the boat, the disciples saw what appeared to be a man coming toward them in the distance walking on water. When the disciples saw him moving in the direction of their boat, they were panic-stricken, thinking they were looking at some kind of demonic ethereal being. Frightened, they cried out, "It's a ghost!" But Peter knew differently. He believed it was Jesus, the Son of God.

Have you ever been in a situation where you encountered an unexpected circumstance? Do you recall feeling frightened? Without warning, you found yourself surrounded by uncertainty and fear. This is what the disciples experienced. One minute everything was fine—they were sleeping peacefully, then they suddenly found themselves in the middle of a terrible storm.

This story is an excellent illustration of how fear can override your faith. Except for Peter, the disciples all reacted emotionally out of fear. Why? How is it that Peter reacted in faith and the other disciples reacted in fear? I believe it has to do with a difference in their core beliefs about Christ. I would imagine the disciples still had doubts about the deity of Jesus deep within their core. That is, if you asked them if they believed in Christ, they would most likely say yes, but when caught off guard in a moment of desperation and panic, the truth about what they believed would surface. However, Peter reacted immediately with faith. Deep within his core, he was certain the man he was following was Jesus Christ, the Son of God. Because of Peter's deep-seated belief about the deity of Christ, his immediate response was faith. He was confident Jesus was the one walking toward them on the water that stormy night.

When Jesus drew close, Peter decided to take a leap of faith. He called out to Jesus, saying, "If it is you tell me to come out to you." Jesus responded, "It is I. Do not be afraid." In the natural, Peter knew what he was about to do was impossible, but, full of faith, he climbed out and walked toward Jesus. I can't imagine how it must have felt to climb out of that boat in the middle of a storm. I would think every one of my internal instincts would fight me to stay in the boat and try to figure a way to stay as safe as possible. But despite instincts, Peter stepped off the ledge into the deep, dark, churning waters with angry waves rising and falling with each gust of wind. It was a miracle. With his initial steps, Peter did not consider the possibility of sinking because he believed deep in his heart Christ would hold him up.

This story, however, takes an interesting turn. The moment Peter took his eyes off of Jesus and noticed the velocity of the wind moving quickly toward him, he suddenly felt afraid. The instant Peter looked away from Jesus and focused his attention on the situation surrounding him, everything changed. He lost faith. At that second, the impossibility of walking on water in the middle of an unpredictable storm seemed more likely than God's ability to perform a miracle. Peter's thoughts, not his faith, took over and caused him to be afraid. I would guess he was saying to himself something along the lines of, *What am I doing? There is no way I can take another step without sinking. This wind will push me under the water, and these turbulent waves will consume me. Walking on water is impossible.* These kinds of thoughts could have easily caused Peter to lose faith in

Christ's ability to do the impossible. Peter became overwhelmed by the elements of the storm and lost sight of the power Christ had to instantly steady the winds and calm the waters.

The storm Peter and the disciples experienced can easily parallel with storms you may encounter within your own life. You simply go about your daily routine when, out of nowhere, an unexpected crisis hits, and you, like Peter and the disciples, catch yourself scrambling to find a way to keep from sinking beneath the waves of your circumstance. You feel uncertain, shaken, and afraid. These feelings are likely connected to a core belief rooted in fear. You could have a fear of failure, a fear of being alone, a fear of being hurt, a fear of the unknown, or an overwhelming fear that you cannot handle the weight of the storm you are facing. Core beliefs rooted in fear can cause you to doubt God's capacity to intervene and do the impossible. It can cause you to question his ability to comfort you and give you hope for a brighter future, or it can persuade you to distrust his willingness to heal your broken heart. Fear is a powerful emotion that influences your beliefs, thoughts, feelings, and behaviors.

THE POWER OF IRRATIONAL FEAR

Irrational fear is a powerful stronghold that can drive you to act in ways motivated by a faulty core belief. This belief convinces you something terrible will happen unless you take control and intervene. It is a belief that is generally rooted in a lie. What lie are you believing? Do you have a fear of being hurt, a fear of someone you love being hurt, a fear of failure, fear of rejection, a fear of abandonment, or a fear of loss?

In chapter 3, I talked about how false beliefs create a faulty filter that pollutes your perception of yourself and any given event in your life. It is not until you cleanse your filtered beliefs and tainted thoughts that your perceptions will change.

Perhaps you have tried to change the way you think and feel but your efforts were of little avail. Regardless of how hard you have tried not to think fearful thoughts or not to doubt God's ability and willingness to answer your prayers, you continue to remain frightened, overwhelmed, and hopeless. Simply telling yourself that you will not feel afraid or think negative thoughts does not usually work. If it were that simple, everyone would have healthy thinking. You have to do the hard work of investigating the core beliefs that have damaged your mental filter.

On the surface, changing your core beliefs seems easy enough, but changing your beliefs requires you to understand their origin and learn how to identify their roots and strongholds. This process can take time and may require a great deal of effort. This chapter will explain how the cycle of core beliefs, thoughts, feelings, reactions, and behaviors work. Once you understand this process, you will be better equipped to identify your core beliefs and challenge those that are false, faulty, and distorted.

IDENTIFYING CORE BELIEFS

When clients would come to me grief-stricken, afraid, or reeling from a painful experience or trauma, they were desperate for answers. They never came into my office asking me to help them uncover the faulty core beliefs they thought contributed to their pain, fear, and hopelessness. They were looking for support and tools to help manage their grief, relieve them of their fear, or discover a way to find hope. All they knew was they felt bad and wanted to feel better. Uncovering faulty beliefs was not part of their plan.

People seek counseling because they feel overwhelmed with sorrow, fear, confusion, anger, regret, and so much more. They want answers. Knowing how to change destructive thinking and faulty core beliefs is the last thing people want when they are suffering. My clients did not come to me because they thought they had terrible thinking or a broken belief system. They came because they felt bad. Everyone will feel bad when something terrible happens, but underneath the "bad" feelings is a core belief system that filters your thoughts and perceptions. If this system is damaged, your thoughts become distorted, significantly affecting how you feel and behave.

Core beliefs are conclusions you have made about things such as who you believe you are, what you determine you are capable of doing or not doing, and how you think you fit into the world surrounding you. They also encompass your convictions about who you believe God is and what you think about others and the world in which you live.

These beliefs are like roots deeply embedded in your mind. Like branches growing out of a tree, your thoughts grow in a similar way. A tree starts with a seed; the seed germinates and grows roots. Fully grown, it has many branches sprouting from its trunk, creating an expansive canopy. Core beliefs work similarly. It starts with an idea; it grows roots and eventually becomes a mature belief with many thoughts branching from the mind arching over like an umbrella.

When clients would come to me suffering and in pain, I was always on the hunt for faulty core beliefs. These beliefs, I knew, motivated their feelings and behaviors, and controlled their emotional reactions. I looked for core beliefs like: *I am damaged . . . I am unlovable . . . I am not good enough . . . I am a failure* . . . and so on. I also looked for my client's false core beliefs about God: *God does not love me . . . God punishes me . . . God is disappointed in me . . . God cannot heal my brokenness.* I would look for faulty core beliefs about my client's perception of others: *People are out to get me . . . People will abandon me . . . People judge me. . . . People are selfish and self-serving . . .* Finally, I would look for false beliefs about their ideas of the world: *The world is evil . . . Life is unfair . . . Bad things will always happen to me . . . I am not safe.*

Because thoughts are strongly influenced by core beliefs deeply rooted in the mind and feelings and behaviors are driven by thoughts, I understood the value of exposing faulty beliefs during counseling. By bringing these beliefs to the surface, my clients would know why they felt and behaved the way they did. It was my job, as their therapist, to help them unravel their thoughts and ideas that contributed to their unwanted, destructive, damaging, or harmful feelings and behaviors.

THE CYCLE OF THE LIE

Most everyone has a set of faulty core beliefs based on lies—lies that lurk beneath the surface. These lies are generally connected to your past. They can be ideas created when you had a particular experience, or they can be ideas you have received from others, especially from individuals who carry importance and merit in your life.

These distorted ideas of the truth create a faulty belief system that influences your thoughts and feelings about what is happening around you. These faulty beliefs often drive your emotional reactions and control the way you feel. There are five main components to this cycle.

1. Core Beliefs and 2. Thoughts

Thoughts and core beliefs are two factors that directly affect each other. For example, you can have thoughts initiated by your core beliefs, and your core beliefs can be influenced, made stronger, or made deeper-seated by your thoughts. For instance:

You had a past experience that created core beliefs: *I was made fun of by other kids at school and my parents and teachers only talked about what I did wrong.*

Your core beliefs: *I believe I am not good enough, not smart enough, I don't measure up, and people don't like me.*

Your thoughts: *I can't do this. This is too hard.*

Here the thought *I can't do this* is initiated by a core belief *I am not good enough.* Because you believe you don't measure up to others, you think you are incompetent, and you tell yourself it is too hard. These thoughts reinforce your core beliefs: *I am not good enough, I am not smart enough, I don't measure up, and people don't like me.* Your thoughts occur in your conscious mind. However, your core beliefs are deep-seated and deeply rooted in your unconscious mind. Your conscious mind is simply the thoughts you are aware of having. Like the thought *I can't do this.* While thinking you can't do something, you may have a series of other conscious thoughts to justify why you can't do something. However, your unconscious mind holds a belief or a series of beliefs you are not aware of having on the surface. It is not until you deliberately take the time to think about what these beliefs are that they will move from your unconscious mind to your conscious thinking.

This cycle has a reciprocal nature between your thoughts and core beliefs. These elements of the cycle go back and forth. Your thoughts are fueled by your core beliefs, and your core beliefs are reinforced by your thoughts. It is similar to putting gasoline into your car. Once your vehicle is filled with gas, the engine is reinforced with the fuel it needs to move forward. Your thoughts and beliefs work in a similar way. When they are reinforced and fueled, they move the cycle of thinking, feeling, and behaving into motion.

3. Feelings

You may think your feelings are the driving force behind your thoughts. You feel inadequate, so you conclude you must be inadequate. But it's the opposite that is true. You think you are incompetent and inferior to others, so you tell yourself certain things are too hard, and you are unable to be successful; as a result, you feel inadequate. Consequently, you give up. It is your conscious thoughts that drive the way you feel. Again, your conscious thoughts are rooted in your unconscious core beliefs. Your core beliefs prompt your thoughts, and these thoughts are what influences, even dictates, your feelings. Because your thoughts determine your feelings, feelings are not predictors of truth.

For example, feelings of inadequacy and shame ultimately stem from your fundamental core beliefs that say, *I am not good enough, I am not smart enough, I do not measure up, and people don't like me.* These core beliefs cause you to think, *I can't do this. This is too hard.* These conscious thoughts that are rooted in your unconscious core beliefs are what make you feel inadequate. This process is why feelings are not facts—they are often the result of negative thinking and false core beliefs.

4. Behaviors

Behaviors are driven by the way you feel, and they also have an impact on your thoughts and core beliefs. For example, when you think something is too difficult, you most likely will not try—not trying causes you to fail, reinforcing your beliefs that you are not good enough. This failure confirms your thoughts about the task being too hard to do and supports your core belief that you are not smart enough. Consequently, the roots of your core beliefs deepen and become stronger.

When you let your feelings dictate your behaviors, you are more likely to self-sabotage. That is, your behaviors will act as a confirmation of your core beliefs, thoughts, and feelings. For example, you are afraid your friend will abandon you. You have a core belief that people you care about will eventually leave you, so you tell yourself not to trust your friends and to keep yourself at a distance. Your core beliefs and thoughts cause you to feel afraid. You think your fear of being abandoned confirms that you cannot trust anyone, but your feelings of fear are not based on truth; they are based on a faulty core belief and fearful thinking. Rather than pushing past your fears by confronting these thoughts and beliefs, you let your fears dictate your behaviors by causing you to act in ways that drive your friend away. When your friend becomes aloof or detached due to your behavior, it confirms your fear of abandonment, reinforcing your core belief that people you care about will eventually leave you.

On the flip side, when you confront your faulty core beliefs, challenge your negative thinking, and push past the way you feel to engage in behaviors where you are successful, your core beliefs are disrupted. You now have new evidence to contradict your faulty core beliefs and negative thinking. These new experiences provoke thoughts that are not rooted in lies and can support a new belief grounded in truth. As a result, you will begin to stop feeling afraid and inadequate. Instead, you will begin feeling hopeful, encouraged, and valued.

5. Reactions

Reactions are not the same as behaviors. Your reactions are automatic responses that are often a direct result of your core beliefs, and your behaviors are a choice based on your thoughts. Reactions result from not thinking, while behaviors are consciously chosen based on your thoughts and conclusions regarding a circumstance. Think about having a reflex. Have you ever been to the doctor when they tap your knee with a rubber hammer in order to get your leg to jump? Your leg's response is an automatic reaction you don't have any control over. The same is true when you find yourself in a situation when something unexpected happens. Before you have had a chance to process what is happening, you react. Later, you may wonder why you reacted the way you did. Reactions generally originate in part, if not entirely, within your deep-seated core beliefs.

Consider this example:

Core Belief: I am not good enough and I am unworthy of love.

Reaction: You get defensive and blame someone or something for your perceived incompetence.

Feelings: Worthlessness

Behavior: You give up easily, or you refuse to try.

Thoughts: I am a loser.

Feelings: Depression

Behavior: Inability to get anything accomplished

Within this cycle, the core belief that you are not good enough and are therefore unworthy of love has been confirmed by your thoughts and behaviors. To understand why you have specific reactions, you must discover the root of your core belief. In this case, it could be an experience or multiple experiences that lead you to the conclusion you are not good enough. Once you have discovered the root, you must extract and remove it in order to heal from the wounds that occurred from your past experiences.

Understanding this cycle can shed light on why you react and behave the way you do in any given set of circumstances. When you have a false core belief that says you are not good enough, it is not surprising if you overreact when you encounter a situation that seems to confirm this lie.

The Cycle of Core Beliefs, Thoughts, Feelings, Reactions, and Behaviors

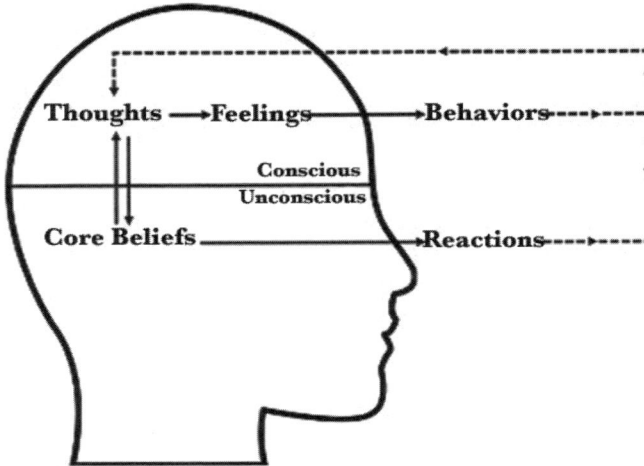

Take a circumstance where a child makes an unintentional mistake: While a brother and sister are arguing, the brother flings his arm in the air, carelessly knocking over a glass bowl sitting on the kitchen counter, which slings shards of glass all over the tile floor. Their mom reacts emotionally by yelling at her son. After yelling, she thinks, *If he had just listened to me when I told him to stop arguing with his sister, this accident would not have happened. Why doesn't he listen to me?* These thoughts are rooted within and subconsciously influenced by her core belief system. She believes, *I will never be a good mom because my kids don't listen to me and they constantly disobey. I never seem to measure up or get it right. I am not good enough, smart enough, or deserving enough.* These faulty core beliefs set the stage for her to overreact in anger when her children's behaviors seem to confirm her false core beliefs.

Reacting in anger, most likely, is subconsciously attached to her faulty core beliefs causing her to automatically yell at her son for being careless. Her beliefs about who she is at her core prompt her emotional reaction of anger. Anger is an emotion that gives an initial sense of power and control. Her core belief is embedded in shame that says, "I am not good enough." These beliefs create just the right chain of events for an emotional reaction of anger.

In addition to causing an emotional reaction, her core beliefs also affect her feelings. When her emotions of anger subside, she feels guilty for shouting. Her feelings of guilt result from her perception of how she thought she should have handled the situation. She thinks, *I should not have raised my voice; maybe this is why my children don't listen to me. If I could remain calm, they would listen. I am a terrible mother. What kind of mom yells at her child for having an accident? I am never going to have their respect. I feel like a failure. I know better.* This manner of negative, self-defeating thinking causes her to feel guilty, reinforcing her core belief: *I am not good enough.* She subconsciously concludes that she not only made a mistake—she is a mistake. Believing she is a mistake is the root of her feelings of shame. The false core belief, *I am not good enough,* creates a negative internal dialogue about herself, causing her to decide her overall performance as a mother does not measure up to her standards of being a good mom.

Before we move on, I want to mention how your emotions play a role in this cycle. Emotions are a specialized subset of reactions that result from a biological subconscious reaction to an event deeply embedded in the framework of your thinking—your core beliefs. They primarily manifest in the form of reactions, as in the case with this mom. Emotions are often confused with feelings. Feelings are your conscious responses to your thoughts and core beliefs. Emotions, on the other hand, are an unconscious reaction. Understanding this difference will clarify why you feel and behave the way you do. This difference can be confusing because these words are used interchangeably in our culture, but they are not the same.

In this example, the mom's feelings of guilt are the result of her thinking she did not handle the situation correctly, and her anger is a subconscious reaction from her core beliefs that she is not good enough. She reacts in anger, but she chooses to feel guilty based on her perception of the event and her thoughts about how she handled the situation. The conscious choice and subconscious reaction have roots embedded within her core belief system. In this case, she believes she is not good enough or, more accurately, she is not a good enough mother.

When she thinks to herself, *I will never be an acceptable mom because my kids don't listen to me, and they constantly disobey,* she is subconsciously on the lookout for evidence to support these thoughts and confirm her core beliefs. When her children act out, she thinks their misbehavior is proof she is not a good mom. Because she believes her children's conduct determines her worth, her worth will always be at the mercy of their behavior. She considers their actions to be a judgment on her performance as a mother; therefore, she thinks she is not good enough when her children's behavior does not satisfy her expectations. As a result of these thoughts, she feels fearful she will never be a good mom if her kids continue to disobey.

Thinking her children do not respect her can quickly spark frustration and anger when they make a careless mistake. Believing she is not good enough will likely cause her to overreact in most situations involving her children's disobedience. When they disobey, she automatically responds without thinking because she has already decided consciously and subconsciously their "bad behavior" confirms her belief that she is an incompetent mother. This core belief sets her up emotionally to react with anger and frustration a lot of the time.

The driving force for this feeling of not being good enough may be powered by other core beliefs such as: *I am a failure of a person, I am letting my kids down, I am letting my husband down,* or *I am an embarrassment.* Remember, core beliefs function like a tree. Once you discover one root, it may lead you to many more. Once you discover a core belief, many other thoughts branch off of these beliefs. When you are trying to understand why you have a certain reaction over and over, it is important that you examine all of the roots that are planted deep in your mind and the branches that grow into a canopy of thoughts.

When I would have clients struggling with unwanted reactions they repeatedly displayed when they were confronted with a stressful or unexpected circumstance, I would search for faulty core beliefs hiding deep beneath the surface that would explain why this reaction occurred over and over. As their therapist, it was my job to help them discover those beliefs, uncover where they originated, and help them dispute and eliminate them from their belief system. It is not until you find out the origin and locate the root of your reactions that you can understand why you react to certain situations the way you do. Once you discover the root, you can begin the work of disputing and challenging your beliefs that a lie or series of lies have either created or contaminated. Understanding the cycle of your thoughts, feelings, and behaviors will help you uncover the core beliefs lurking beneath the surface of your conscious mind.

If you are repeatedly experiencing an unwanted reaction, become your own detective. Look for the lies lurking deep within your core, and ask yourself, What is at the root? Think about experiences you may have had or lies you have believed that have created or influenced your core beliefs. Once you discover your false core beliefs, begin disputing them and challenge their validity. Challenging core beliefs is a journey, not a sprint. It may take you some time to rethink and relearn a new healthier belief system. Be persistent and be patient.

EXPOSING THE LIE BEHIND YOUR FEELINGS

Taking a closer look at your thoughts and core beliefs will enable you to move forward toward healing. Ignoring or refusing to examine what you believe deep within your core will keep you stuck. When you consider your feelings as facts and allow them to be the driving force behind your behavior, you often become unable to move ahead in your journey toward emotional healing. For example, making decisions from a place of fear rather than faith can cause you to become paralyzed and unable to move toward a healthy solution because you convince yourself it is too risky or too hard, so you do nothing. Moving forward requires you to examine the root of your fear and challenge the lies that lie beneath the surface. Looking past your pain to expose the lies that may exist within your core belief system will enable you to take control of your thoughts and better manage your feelings and behavior.

Examining your core beliefs may require you to look beyond your wounds and brokenness. Often when you are hurting, it is difficult to think of anything else, much less buried beliefs that may contribute to the degree to which you are suffering. Having the willingness and the courage to set your heartache aside to do the work of discovering your core beliefs and their roots will put you on the path to healing.

Have you ever gone to an escape room? My family and I love them! We enjoy the challenge of figuring out the clues and trying to escape successfully within the allotted time. When you enter the room, you are locked in with no obvious way of getting out. It isn't until you look for and solve a series of riddles and clues that you can find your way of escape. Once all of the clues have been figured out, you can solve the mystery and unlock the door.

Looking for beliefs that are not grounded in the truth is like being in an escape room. You are locked into a particular way of thinking and feeling, and you have to look for clues to understand why you think and feel the way you do. To experience freedom, you have to solve the mystery and find the root of why you think, feel, and behave the way you do. It isn't until you find and understand the root cause of your pain that you can unlock the door to emotional freedom. Underneath your conscious thoughts are unconscious beliefs that directly affect and influence your feelings. It is essential to figure out what you believe at your core to change the way you feel.

REMOVING THE LIE

When uncovering the lies deep within your mind, you are looking for beliefs not grounded in truth. They are distorted beliefs rooted in soil that has been tainted by either your past experiences or by ideas you received from other people in your life. They are lies you have accepted as truth. These flawed interpretations of the truth are the faulty core beliefs hidden beneath the surface of your thoughts, feelings, and behaviors.

To discover your core beliefs, ask yourself what you believe to be true about yourself, God, and others. The Bible serves as a guide to compare your core beliefs against God's Word. When you see a discrepancy, acknowledge you are accepting a lie as truth. Exposing false core beliefs will help you see your circumstances from a different perspective.

For example, if you have decided in your core that God cannot heal your broken heart and does not really care about you, look at what the Bible says about God's love for you and his ability to heal those he loves. Psalm 103:2–4 says, "Bless the LORD, O my soul, and forget not all his benefits, who forgives all your iniquity, who heals all your diseases, who redeems your life from the pit, who crowns you with steadfast love and mercy" (ESV). Psalm 147:3 explains, "He heals the brokenhearted and binds up their wounds." Finally, James 5:16 asserts, "Therefore, confess your sins to one another and pray for one another, that you may be healed" (ESV).

All of these passages confirm God loves you and is your healer. Believing God does not care about you makes you think you are a target for bad things to happen. Because of the lie—*He doesn't love me, and he will not heal my brokenness*—you assign God with the intention of not caring. Your false core belief taints your idea about who God is. Removing this belief will enable you to see God differently—truthfully.

Rather than thinking, *He doesn't care, and he won't heal me from my pain,* first acknowledge God's Word says something completely different. Then trust his Word contains the truth. Finally, challenge your false belief about God, eventually replacing the lie with the truth. Removing this belief will enable you to see God differently. You no longer believe God doesn't care. Instead, you accept God is, in fact, your healer, and he genuinely loves you.

When you read God's Word, it arms you with the ability to expose the lies within your mind. Understanding the truth in the Bible will expose those hidden faulty core beliefs. By contrasting your beliefs against Scripture, you learn to discern truth and understand that God loves you no matter your circumstance. When you feel discouraged, God's Word can change your perspective. Recognizing your faulty core beliefs will initiate a change in your beliefs and your feelings about who God is.

When considering the truth of God's Word, there are many different beliefs you can have that constitute a lie. For example, believing you are not good enough goes directly against what we read in the Bible:

"Therefore, if anyone is in Christ, he is a new creation. The old has passed away; behold, the new has come" (2 Corinthians 5:17 ESV). Paul was explaining your worth is not based on your past, your performance, your success, or your failures. Your value comes from the redeeming blood of Jesus. When you accept him into your heart, he cleanses you and makes you into a new creation. You are redeemed, and with redemption comes worth and value. Your value is no longer attached to your performance but to the bloodline of Christ. Your worth is in him! Reading God's Word and understanding the truths he teaches arms you with the ability to expose the lies within your core beliefs.

Some of the lies I see most frequently are:

I am damaged goods.

I am unlovable.

I am not good enough.

I am unacceptable.

I am a failure.

I am afraid everyone I love will leave me.

God does not care about me.

God is punishing me.

God cannot be pleased.

God is not fair.

God cannot heal my brokenness.

God cannot change my circumstance.

People always judge me.

People don't care about me.

People are out to get me.

People are selfish.

The world is evil.

Life is unfair.

Life is not worth living.

Something bad is going to happen.

Being wrong will expose my incompetence.

Everything has to go my way for me to feel okay.

My way is the best way—the only way.

When I am in control, I cannot be hurt.

These are just some samples of the lies embedded in the minds of many. Clinging to any of these false core beliefs will cloud, distort, and impair your judgment. These lies will cause you to see your circumstances from an inaccurate and misleading perspective.

LOOKING FOR EVIDENCE

Often, false core beliefs are difficult to dispute and challenge because of the evidence you think you find to support them. Have you ever heard of the term *confirmation bias?* Confirmation bias looks for proof within your circumstances that supports an idea, perception, or opinion. It is the tendency to focus on information that endorses your beliefs and minimizes evidence that may disprove them. Confirmation bias causes your overall perception to become tainted by the evidence you think you find supporting an idea likely rooted in a lie. You see this in politics quite often.

The lies that exist within your core belief system are on the lookout for an indication of support. For example, losing a loved one may confirm a false belief of abandonment. This loss seems to endorse your fear of being left all alone. When the loss occurs, you may tell yourself: *I knew this would happen, I cannot trust people to stay around, I should have never let myself love them, I will never be in a relationship again,* or *I cannot let go, I cannot live without them, my life is incomplete . . .* These thoughts solidify the lie, "People will abandon me. I cannot trust them to stay around."

When you have these kinds of deep-seated thoughts, becoming vulnerable and trusting others seems unthinkable. This kind of thinking can lead you to believe a loss of a loved one is the evidence you need to support your fears of being left alone. This kind of faulty thinking will motivate you to avoid intimacy with others by either erecting impenetrable emotional walls or deliberately sabotaging any relationships you may have. Each time someone leaves you, your false belief of being abandoned grows deeper roots. You decide your only protection against being left alone is keeping everyone at arm's length.

However, a failure to find evidence can provoke you to create the proof you need to support your core belief by creating a self-fulfilling prophecy. A self-fulfilling prophecy is much like predicting the future. When you believe a lie about yourself, someone else, or a feared event, you behave in ways that will bring to pass this deceptive presumption.

For example, many of my abused clients believed they were victims long after the abuse had ended. Their core belief said, "People will always mistreat and hurt me." In relationships, they refused to set boundaries allowing others to take advantage of them. Saying no, they believed, was nearly impossible. These behaviors created the evidence they needed to conclude they would always be a victim. This pattern would present itself in various forms in every relationship, whether it was a friendship, a coworker, or a family member.

Because they believed they were victims, they behaved like victims, causing people to mistreat them. Their inability to say no and to set boundaries led others to treat them poorly. Their failure to behave differently invited the mistreatment of others, making their belief about being a victim a self-fulfilling prophecy that served as "proof" of their false belief that "People will always hurt me."

Others of my abused clients maintained they were also doomed to be victims but had other lies attached to this belief. As a whole these clients believed they did not deserve to be loved, and it was up to them to protect themselves at all costs from letting anyone hurt them. While on the surface this may not seem like a lie, upon closer inspection, this false core belief promoted behaviors that kept my clients far removed from any kind of intimacy in relationships. These individuals became over-controlling and did not allow anyone to get too close. They concluded that feeling alone, empty, and isolated was the price they had to pay to protect themselves. At their core, most all of them universally believed they were undeserving of unconditional love. My particular clients' controlling and isolating behavior fulfilled the prophecy they were unlovable victims.

Looking for evidence to support false core beliefs can be a significant stumbling block to emotional healing. To move forward, you have to identify and recognize when you are using a confirmation bias and creating a self-fulfilling prophecy. Becoming aware of this behavior will help you look for evidence that challenges the lies within your core beliefs rather than finding evidence that supports them. Focus on the evidence that contradicts the faulty core belief and allow that evidence to be a substantial reason to create a new core belief. Once you expose the lies and replace them with truth, your spiritual foundation is strengthened. As a result, you are more prepared to sustain the turbulent winds when an unexpected storm finds its way into your life.

EXPECTING THE UNEXPECTED

If you have a core belief system that has been contaminated with lies, you are vulnerable to becoming overwhelmed and consumed by fear. As

I mentioned earlier, we see this kind of fearful reaction in the lives of the disciples when Jesus walked toward them on the water during a terrible storm. The disciples all reacted in fear, whereas Peter reacted in faith. Remember, reactions are automatic and are almost always connected to a core belief. Because of his solid belief that Jesus Christ was the true Messiah, Peter was prepared for the storm. However, he most likely had other core beliefs that were vulnerable to being challenged. When Peter took his eyes off of Jesus, his thoughts took a turn, and he felt afraid. Peter became distracted by the circumstances that surrounded him—the wind and the waves. These unpredictable and contentious elements of the storm became his focus. Even after you have done the work of lining up your core beliefs with the Word of God, there will still be unexpected situations and circumstances that will challenge and shake you at your core. Unrelenting thoughts beat up against your mind like torrential rain crashing on the roof of your home, telling you over and over you will not survive. Your focus shifts and you suddenly become consumed by the elements that surround you, so you call into question your beliefs. This kind of cross-examination of your belief system can be considered a crisis in faith.

This is what happened to me. I found myself questioning God's ability to show up and intervene in a supernatural way that summer after Tori's freshman year in college.

Despite my strong and secure beliefs, I found myself challenging them at their very core. I knew God loved me and was capable of intervening, but when I desperately cried out for God to help my daughter and nothing changed, I started believing a lie. I told myself nothing was ever going to change, and my daughter was gone forever. I took my eyes off him and focused on what was happening all around me. Fear consumed me. I wanted to give up on God because he seemed a million miles away. I started believing the lie that he was not going to intervene because I prayed every day for him to show up, but every day things got worse, not better. I encountered a faith crisis. I lost sight of who God was amid my crisis. It wasn't until I looked away from my situation and focused on the nature of God did my perspective start to change. During Tori's long journey to recovery, I had to let go of my fear and trust God had a plan. Despite how I was feeling I had to look to the character of God and not to the cruelty of my circumstance. Believing God is a good God even in the midst of an unexpected storm was key for me to have hope beyond my heartache. I learned to depend on him and not on the prognosis of my daughter's illness. His strength and supernatural power are what got me through. For Tori, staying steadfast, being determined, and having faith in a God who is bigger than any circumstance is how she overcame that storm. His faithfulness is now fully realized in her life.

STAYING ON COURSE

When considering loss or walking through a painful circumstance, fear can often threaten your beliefs about your ability to overcome and God's ability to intervene. It is the one feeling that can stop you dead in your tracks. Fear creates a dialogue within your mind convincing you of its necessity. It looks for ways to intimidate you into believing its lies and tries to convince you there is a reason to be afraid. The only way to go beyond this kind of fear is to examine whether it is a valid fear or a lie embedded in your core beliefs. Having the ability to dispute and challenge your fearful thoughts and false core beliefs will help you move away from irrational fear and toward faith.

Creating a firm foundation in the knowledge of God's Word will equip you with this ability. For Peter, his faith in Jesus gave him the courage to step out of the boat. You, too, can step out of your boat and into the unknown, trusting God will calm the waters and keep you from sinking. However, while walking in faith, you must keep your eyes focused on Jesus because fearful thinking will try to emerge and steer you off course, causing you to look away and sink. When I turned my eyes toward Jesus during that awful storm of Tori's illness, I experienced a supernatural peace that gave me hope and courage to keep moving forward. That experience happened five years ago, and today Tori lives a happy and fulfilling life. She has not had another episode. She is a fighter and works diligently to stay healthy and strong! God did have a plan, and now it is easy to see in the rearview mirror. In the midst of the storm, though, I was blinded by all of the flooding rains. It took faith and courage to set aside my fears and look to God for direction even when I thought I was going to sink. I had to look beneath the surface and identify the lies I believed that caused me to doubt God. I had to examine what I truly believed about God and myself, so I read the Bible looking for truth and for his promises of healing.

I read, "For I am the LORD, who heals you" (Exodus 15:26); "I will give you back your health and heal your wounds" (Jeremiah 30:17 NLT); "So do not fear, for I am with you; do not be dismayed, for I am your God. I will strengthen you and help you; I will uphold you with my righteous right hand" (Isaiah 41:10). His Word was like a salve on an open wound. It comforted me and soothed the aching in my soul. God is the one who enabled me to see past the storm and have faith everything would work for a greater purpose.

HELPFUL TOOLS

1. When you have a reaction you do not like or understand, what might be the root of it all? Journal about the experience and try to determine the belief that prompted the reaction.

2. Ask yourself what you believe about yourself and record your thoughts in your journal. Determine if these beliefs line up with truth. Write out the beliefs you think need to be disputed.

3. Ask yourself what you believe about God and record your thoughts in your journal. Determine if these beliefs line up with truth. Write out the beliefs you think need to be disputed.

4. Ask yourself what you believe about others and record your thoughts in your journal. Determine if these beliefs line up with truth. Write out the beliefs you think need to be disputed.

5. Ask yourself what you believe about the world and record your thoughts in your journal. Determine if these beliefs line up with truth. Write out the beliefs you think need to be disputed.

6. Write out thoughts you have frequently that are either negative thoughts or thoughts that do not line up with the truth.

7. Replace your negative thoughts with a new perspective. Allow this new viewpoint to create a more positive line of thinking based on the truth of God's Word.

6
A Cup of Sorrow
How to Embrace Your Feelings

I've lost the baby."

Not long ago my friend Miranda went to the hospital expecting to return home with her long-awaited newborn cradled in her arms.

Now she was home, empty-handed and empty-hearted.

I couldn't imagine the depth of her sorrow. How could this happen to such a kind, loving person? Miranda always wanted to have a child of her own. Even though she struggled for years to get pregnant, she still found ways to nurture other people's children. As a special education teacher for autistic students, her love for them was obvious to anyone who knew her well. She always affectionately referred to them as "my kids."

When she announced to our weekly Bible study group that she was expecting, we were thrilled. We cheered and celebrated this new beginning for Miranda, which was the answer to so many of our prayers. Finally, she began to live her dream and her heart's desire.

She was sick and fatigued through most of her pregnancy, but she never complained. She kept a positive attitude and made it to our study every week, encouraging us in our faith and growing alongside us. She worked hard to do all the right things to stay in good health, from eating well and exercising, to taking vitamins. She read up on what to expect during pregnancy and how to handle early child development. She was excited and ready, and we were so happy for her.

Now this. So devastating. I wanted to reach out, offer some comfort. *But what can I say to possibly make a difference?* I wondered. *Maybe I should wait and give her time.*

This is what we do when the worst happens. We hesitate. We isolate. We often don't say anything in fear of saying the wrong thing. Sometimes we do even worse. We say something that hurts.

Once, I was facilitating a group therapy session for women recovering from past trauma and abuse. The women were at different stages in their recovery, and their experiences and circumstances varied. But the pain, trauma, and scars were universal, which made what one woman said in a group session so alarming.

"Haven't you grieved long enough?" she sniped to another woman who had just painfully shared about a deep loss. "It's time for you to get over it."

The words hung in the air. It felt like gravity had been sucked from the room and each of us in the circle were suddenly untethered in space, weightless, adrift, and trying not to bump into those awful meteors of pain and hurt.

Stunned, no one spoke for what seemed like minutes. Such bold insensitivity knocked the air out of us. Then the sound of my own heart pounding startled me back to my senses.

This was not okay. It was up to me as the facilitator, the "therapist," to address the casualty of her selfish and provoking words. Careless words are often the result of other people's attempts to convince themselves they are in control of someone else's feelings. These individuals actually think their heartless words will help. They believe tough love is the answer. Though misguided, their intention is to stop the hurt. They want to remove the overwhelming feelings of despair. But I have learned feelings need not be stopped but rather validated and affirmed. Knowing someone sees you, hears you, and allows you the space to feel is often the first step in moving past your feelings of devastation and despair.

That was the cry of Miranda's heart: *Please someone stop the hurt.*

When faced with crises feelings are often what take over your life. As a cognitive therapist, I was trained to concentrate solely on individuals' thoughts and beliefs, but I learned differently from watching my daughter Tori become paralyzed by the way she felt. Her feelings were so debilitating that trying to change the way she thought was often not the first course of action. It was futile. I realized the importance of her learning to validate and tend to how she felt was essential to her receiving inner healing. Because feelings manifest themselves in different ways with different people, it is essential to not criticize or judge someone when they might be stuck.

In this chapter, it is my goal to momentarily set aside the strategies used to challenge and dispute your irrational and faulty beliefs and thoughts long enough to give your emotions a voice. Oftentimes when you are overcome by crises and heartbreak, the intensity of your emotions is what takes front and center, and if you do not tend to them often your ability to manage your thoughts and feelings spins you out of control.

YOU FEEL WHAT YOU FEEL

No one looks forward to hard circumstances, loss, and pain. No one likes holding that cup, let alone swallowing the bitter things life serves. When something terrible happens, you feel waves of emotions like you never had before: deep sadness, devastation, despair, anger, hopelessness, frustration, confusion, fear, shame, and doubt. Feelings can wash over you all at once or in cycles, like the tides of an ocean. You can feel engulfed, overwhelmed, undone, and overcome.

As time passes, maybe the people in your circle of work, home, church, and community feel pulled down by your feelings too. Perhaps someone tells you, "It's time to move on." Or "You cannot grieve forever." This could be someone you know and love the most rather than some stranger you recently met in group therapy. Even good-hearted people who really care about you say things like this all the time. They think they're helping. They don't want to see you drown in your sadness, anger, or depression, so they try to hold you up. They add things like, "There's a reason," or "All things work together for the good," or "Let go and let God so you can get on with your life."

But these things don't encourage. Instead, you feel patronized or wounded in the house of friends. As you sink deeper into whatever you're feeling, someone might say, "Isn't it time you get over it?" And whether they meant well or they were simply being selfish and irresponsible, the words sting, because you've probably wondered this for yourself. You ask yourself, *Why can't I move past this unbearable pain?*

Or maybe you have decided you simply won't get over the awful thing that happened, and that's that. Now new feelings wash over you. Shame. Condemnation. More hurt. More regret. *I'm doing it wrong*, you tell yourself. *I'm the problem.*

Emotions and feelings can have such power over us, such control. It can feel like you are desperately trying to outrun a spinning tornado, but you are overtaken by the massive force of the twisting wind. When slammed to the ground, your emotions have succeeded in getting your attention. The aftermath of this emotional cyclone dictates your behavior.

Your feelings can take precedence and first priority over your rationale, clouding what's true in a situation. They're like that loud person at the party, talking over logic, shutting down reason. They can drive you to behave badly or act a little crazy by lashing out at others or doing things that hurt you and alienate the very people who love you.

That doesn't mean emotions are bad. They don't make you incompetent, unstable, or flawed—just human, honest, and real. Feeling something means you have a heart, you're alive, you can heal, grow, and go on.

So before you beat yourself up for what you feel (or let anyone else beat you up), know that your emotions are not good or bad. They just are. You feel what you feel and that's okay. In fact, emotions and feelings are not only okay but also necessary indicators and clues to help you understand why you react or behave a certain way. Understanding and knowing how to deal with your feelings and emotions is an instrumental tool in helping you achieve mental and emotional well-being.

This awareness of your emotions helps you recognize the ebb and flow of strong feelings and helps you understand what situations warrant certain emotions and their given intensity. What may seem out of range to you may be perfectly normal to someone else given the context of their past and present experiences.

When you are faced with overwhelming emotions, decide if your responses to them are reasonable and valid. This will let you know if your emotions are connected to thoughts and beliefs about the triggering event. For example, you feel so depressed you cannot get out of bed. Asking yourself what events or thoughts your feelings of depression are connected to will help you know if this depression makes sense or if it is invalid. If you are grieving the loss of a loved one, it makes sense to feel intense sadness that causes you to feel depressed. In this case, depressed feelings are warranted. If you are depressed because of an unmet expectation of someone not doing something you expected them to do, then feeling depressed over the unmet expectation would not be warranted.

Emotions come in levels of intensity—they are high, low, or some-where in between. When feeling depressed over the loss of a loved one, the intensity of this emotion will most likely be high. You may feel suffocated by your grief and sorrow. Getting out of bed seems to be a herculean task. Being impatient, judgmental, or burdened by feelings of guilt about these feelings will not help you move past them; instead, it will keep you stuck. When you know your feelings are justified, it will help you sit with them long enough for you to feel validated. Once you feel validated you increase your willingness to move forward.

If you are feeling depressed over an unmet expectation, on the other hand, the intensity of that emotion should be low. A low-intensity emotion looks more like irritation or disappointment. Feelings of dis-appointment are valid, but feeling so disappointed you cannot get out of bed is not a reasonable emotional response to an unmet expectation. The reaction is out of range given the circumstance. Understanding your emotional response in terms of intensity will help you know if your feel-ings are valid or not valid.

When you have a high-intensity response to a low-intensity event, the intense emotional response is most likely connected to thoughts and beliefs about something deeper. This is when you will need to change your thinking in order to have a different emotional reaction. Changing an emotional response can take a great deal of time and effort because you are essentially rewiring your brain, so be patient in the process.

FEELINGS AND EMOTIONS

Feelings are based upon individual perception and interpretation; how you view them and think about them makes a difference on how you experience them. Interpretations and perceptions are deeply personal—

as different and diverse as every tiny snowflake. While it is true all snowflakes are white and frozen, they are still very different. Likewise, feelings all have similarities but are unique to the individual.

Feelings describe a conscious reaction to an emotional state. We use the word *feelings* as a more general term to indicate how we experience the world around us, including our emotions. Emotions, on the other hand, result from the brain's reaction to certain signals in the environment. These signals cause biological changes in the body, such as increased heart rate, fatigue, dizziness, sweating, nausea, and panic. While we may use these terms interchangeably, emotions are influenced by the subconscious mind, and their biological reactions may be uncontrollable. Adversely, feelings are purely conscious and may be controlled by our thoughts and actions.

All of our feelings start with our own personal perceptions about a given situation. Everything we experience, including our emotions, initially sifts through our mind, creating a thought, belief, and perception. Your perceptions are the result of various factors, including your past experiences, your upbringing, and your personal belief system or worldview. This is why everyone will have a variety of different reactions to similar situations, why two people can experience the same event but walk away with separate accounts of what happened.

Since we all have different experiences and feelings, we cannot say to a person, "It is time for you to get over it." For some, grieving is a lifelong process. This does not mean you are unable to move on; in fact, you are able to move past your intense emotions. It means your intensity changes over time. It's a matter of finding solace and purpose in the midst of your loss without living the rest of your life feeling like your bones are wasting away.

Learning to bring your intensity down is a skill that will help you move forward. Engaging in self-soothing activities is a great way to calm your emotional intensity. You can take a long bath, listen to relaxing music, write your thoughts and feelings in a journal, or go for a walk. Do whatever it is that will calm your emotions and soothe your hurt.

While others may attempt to understand the way you feel, your feelings are your own personal experience. They are unique to you. How could anyone possibly know exactly how you feel or even why you feel things? Likewise, no one will heal in the same way or in the same amount of time as you. We are all different, distinct, unique individuals who feel and emote differently.

RUNNING AWAY FROM YOUR FEELINGS

While your feelings may seem overwhelming at times, trying to either run away from them or bury them is not the pathway to healing. If you bury or run away from your feelings, you begin to feel numb—a welcome relief to pain, you may say—but this is not the way out. You may be telling yourself it is better to not feel. But even though you are disconnected from your feelings, you are still having an emotional response to your suppressed pain. Understanding your response helps you identify how you cope. For example, numbness is an emotional response. It can also become a coping mechanism. I saw this frequently with my clients who were suffering from past trauma. They believed if they could keep themselves from feeling anything too deeply, they would not have to feel any pain at all.

The problem with being unable to face your feelings is you develop an inability to take risks and be vulnerable in relationships with others. You tell yourself it is better to keep your distance. While it is true you may reduce your risk of getting hurt by others, it also costs you the ability to have any intimate, close, and authentic relationships with others as well. Numbing yourself from the reality of your pain is not a solution but a stumbling block—yet another layer added to the fortress you are building to protect yourself. But at what cost?

FACING YOUR EMOTIONS

Until you allow yourself to experience your feelings, whatever they are, you cannot move past them. Your feelings and emotions are a direct path to your heart, and until you acknowledge, embrace, and understand them, your heart will not be able to completely heal. The awareness of your emotions will give you insight into what you believe, fear, or worry about. They will also give insight to what you distrust, dread, hope for, anticipate, or think about regarding your circumstance. Honestly facing your feelings and allowing yourself to have them with no judgment is an important step to acceptance and to moving forward in your journey. So how do you know what feelings you are experiencing? To understand your feelings, you have to recognize which emotion you are dealing with by being mindful of the notable qualities that characterize each one.

- **Anger:** Anger can range anywhere from irritation or grumpiness to outrage and hostility. Anger can be triggered by physical pain or as a result of other intense emotions such as sadness or fear. When you become angry, you often tell yourself, *Things shouldn't be this way*, or *This is unfair.* You may become hot and sweaty and want to yell and scream. Sometimes anger helps you get what you want, so you give in to this emotion over and over. However, anger can cause numbness and narrowing of your attention, so you tend to ruminate on what made you angry, which directly affects how you feel and how you act toward others.

- **Sadness:** Sadness can be an intense emotion, especially when you are experiencing a loss. It often makes you feel some level of anger toward life, yourself, or others. At a low intensity, sadness looks like disappointment or despondency, and at a high intensity it looks like depression and despair. This emotion causes you to retreat inward and fixate on negative thoughts, which causes you to forget the things that make you happy. It even makes you forget all your pleasant memories, leaving you feeling hopeless and distraught. Sadness can make you feel empty and hollow inside as well as tired and run down. You start to believe life is meaningless, and you think it is impossible to overcome these feelings. You feel misunderstood because no one understands your pain. This emotion causes feelings of helplessness and self-contempt. You start to blame and criticize yourself for feeling this way.

- **Fear:** Fear is an emotion that causes you to feel threatened or out of control in some kind of way. You may be afraid something bad is going to happen or you will be abandoned by someone you love. Fear is also another potential high-intensity emotion. At its highest, you feel intense anxiety, panic, or terror. At the lower end of intensity, you may feel a sense of dread, apprehension, or uneasiness. These emotions make you feel like running away. You may want to scream, yell, or cry; or you may feel like hiding or avoiding the very thing you fear. You physically feel an increase in your heart rate. You may experience nausea or feel an urge to flee or cry out. You may feel cold or clammy with the hairs on the back of your arms or neck standing up. You lose your ability to focus and will often ruminate about how you are feeling.

- **Shame:** Shame is the emotion that makes you feel worthless and damaged. It is the sense that you don't measure up because there is something wrong with you. It is believing you are unlovable and defective. You presume you are inferior to others, thinking you are not good enough. You generally feel self-conscious. This emotion varies in intensity, and most react to it with withdrawal and self-loathing. You may also respond with avoiding behaviors, dodging people, and evading situations that create feelings of shame. Shame can cause you to have an upset stomach or a feeling of dread that takes over your senses. You may shut down and block everything out, distract, or even dissociate.

In the moment, emotions can seem overpowering. They can feel as though they have the ability to take you under. This is when it is essential to lean into your faith. Knowing who God is and understanding his character will help you surrender your heart to him.

In the Old Testament, we are introduced to a young, passionate, and courageous shepherd boy who turned to God whenever he experienced intense emotions. Because he did so, God called him a man after God's own heart.

THE LONELY SHEPHERD BOY

On many occasions David found himself struggling with feelings of disappointment, anger, devastation, and hopelessness. David endured a number of tragedies throughout his life, and heartache often overcame him. His peers and even his very own family harshly rejected him, and David spent many frightening nights hiding from a vengeful king, battling severe anguish over his sin, and fighting the unbearable feeling of being far from God. With each heartbreak, he plummeted into the depths of his sorrow, but David never got stuck. Why?

David was born into a large family in the small town of Bethlehem where he grew up tending sheep and on occasion killing lions and bears to protect his flock. As he mastered the challenges of the unexpected prey, he grew into a strong warrior who against all odds killed a giant named Goliath. As the years went by, he became stronger and more courageous, defeating enemy after enemy. He led armies, and then the nation of Israel.

As a young teenage boy, David was anointed to become king by Samuel, a leader and well-known prophet at the time. After this anointing, he was summoned to play the harp for the current king, Saul. David soon became a familiar face in the king's courts; he even developed a close brotherly friendship with Jonathan, the king's son, and eventually married Saul's daughter Michal.

Destined as a young boy to do God's work, David was filled with the Spirit of God when he wrote poetry, sang, and played his harp. King Saul loved David, especially when he played music. His playing of the harp calmed the king's mind and soothed his irritability and misery.

As he spent hours sitting in his court playing and singing, David had a front-row seat into the life of the king. Saul was so taken by David he appointed him as his armor bearer. It was during this time David killed Goliath. After such a marked victory, Saul selected David to be a warrior and later appointed him commander of his army.

As commander, David successfully led his troops to victory after victory. Upon David's arrival from battle the women sang, "Saul has slain his thousands, and David his tens of thousands" (1 Samuel 18:7). As these words flooded the courts, jealousy weaseled its way into Saul's heart. Saul did not expect David to become so popular. In fact, his popularity threatened Saul. He was afraid David would overthrow him as reigning king, so he banished him from his kingdom.

Once the king sought to kill him, David became a man on the run. He hid in the wilderness and in caves. The most powerful man in the kingdom shunned and rejected him and hunted him down. Feeling like an outcast was familiar to David, a man born into a Jewish family wrought with controversy.

When David was young, he was left alone to tend the sheep out in the fields, so he quickly learned what it felt like to be in isolation for long periods of time. Being expected as a boy to live among the sheep would seem as if David was cast aside by his father and seen as more lowly than his siblings.

I imagine it was in the fields separated from his mother and father where, as a young boy, David began to write. I am sure he wrote about what it felt like to be rejected and overlooked. He was just an innocent boy who struggled with understanding why he was not good enough, why his family seemed to have cast him aside. He was left there in the fields alone; his only companions were his sheep.

I believe he found solace, relief, and comfort in his writing and music. The solitude in the fields taught him the value of self-expression. He conveyed his feelings in an effort to understand and accept his lonely fate. At this tender young age, David learned the importance of acknowledging and validating his feelings of grief and despair.

David wrote not only about his feelings of heartache but also about the beauty of the land that hedged him in while caring for his sheep. While tending his flock, David saw firsthand the majesty of God in the beauty that surrounded him. He experienced God's enduring love, mercy, and grace.

When David called out to God to rescue him from his overwhelming feelings of sorrow, God was there. God became his refuge and hiding place. The wilderness became his home. It was here in the midst of God's beauty, surrounded by the warmth of his presence, David fell in love with his Creator. Being a shepherd boy was the beginning of David's journey of learning how to trust in God to be his comforter, defender, and healer.

Then David found himself as a grown man—anointed to become king—but rejected, alienated, and afraid, alone once again with his thoughts in the depths of the wilderness. What did David do? Did he give up? Did he lose faith in God? Did he die in his despair? No. David did what he knew he needed to do, what he had learned to do as a young shepherd boy. He ran to God, surrendered, cried out for mercy, and then wrote some of the most powerful and moving psalms that bring us comfort even today in our own times of sorrow and despair.

When we read the words David penned, we can clearly see he understood the personhood of God. He knew who God was. He knew God was all-knowing, all-powerful, faithful, holy, and sovereign. He recognized God's workmanship in the beauty that surrounded him. Whether in moments of doubt or fulfillment, he experienced God's strength, power, and wisdom. Throughout his life, he embraced God's unfailing love, peace, and comfort. This is why David kept moving forward, even in the midst of heartache and crises.

ROLLER COASTER OF EMOTIONS

Emotions can catch us off guard. One day you think you have everything under control, and then the next day you are falling apart. Have you ever ridden a roller coaster in the dark? There is a ride at Disney World called Space Mountain. I remember the first time I rode it while in college. I had no idea the ride was in the dark—I was completely unprepared. I had never been so frightened. Because I could not see anything, I couldn't brace myself for what was coming next. All I could do was hold on and hope for the best.

I had no idea if we were going to take a quick turn to the right or to the left, and when the ride would go up a hill, I thought we were going to go straight down only for the ride to take a turn instead. The anticipation of the drop created an immense amount of anxiety for me. I had already decided in my mind the ride was going to take a quick, steep plunge downward, so I took a deep breath and grabbed on tight anticipating the sudden drop that never happened.

My middle daughter, Tori, recently learned she has mild sleep apnea. There are many days where she feels overly tired, which makes it difficult to have enough energy to be productive. When she begins to feel overwhelmed by her tiredness, she initially thinks, *I'm going to be drained and feel bad all day.* She then becomes overwhelmed with sadness and gets sucked into an emotional vortex of depressing emotions, all because she has told herself this is how she is going to feel the rest of the day. But often, as depression is starting to set in, something unexpected happens. She receives an encouraging email, is invited to coffee with a friend, hears an uplifting song, or reads something inspiring. It's much like the roller-coaster ride—she's all prepared to drop straight down when suddenly the ride takes a quick turn, changing her emotional response to what is happening. Emotions, perceptions, and unconscious beliefs work hand in hand, making it challenging to predict what you may feel next. Emotions can be unpredictable.

When walking through a crisis, it can seem like out of nowhere you are hit with an onslaught of unexpected feelings that send you reeling. This is the roller-coaster ride of emotions you so often experience when you are walking through a painful or difficult circumstance. One minute you are fine, but the next you are not.

Maybe you hear a song on the radio, and a heaviness and a sadness washes over you as you are pulled into a memory you did not expect to have. You're melancholic the rest of the day. Or maybe you find yourself in a group of women, and someone starts talking about her baby and you suddenly burst into tears. Or possibly, when preparing dinner after a stressful day at work, with your children arguing and your husband late getting home, you cannot get the can opener to work. Out of frustration you overreact and throw the can onto the floor, spilling red beans everywhere. You then run to your room, slam the door, and fall onto your bed feeling like you cannot go on another day. You wonder, *Where did all that anger come from?*

RIDING THE ROLLER COASTER

Having a roller coaster of emotions reminds me of David. Being a man who came from humble beginnings, he learned early on he would have to lean in and trust God to give him strength, hope, and perseverance. As a poet and a writer who wrote with enormous conviction, he understood the power behind his feelings and the need to express them. He experienced many tragedies and hardships throughout his life, some self-inflicted and others not. With each tragedy, David experienced his feelings to the fullest, and he wrote about them in the book of Psalms. There were occasions when David seemed as though he was "up" one minute and "down" the next. In one breath he was praising God, and in the next he couldn't imagine how he could go on another day.

David didn't just experience his feelings casually; he experienced them deeply, passionately, and to the fullest extent. When he was over-joyed, he danced in the streets. When he was anguished, he tore his clothes and refused to eat. When he was afraid, he ran and hid in caves. He didn't just feel things in brief, shallow waves; he went under with each one, became undone, washed up, emptied, and dried out. All of this from the man made just as God intended, exactly as God designed. He felt so much that he wrote an entire book chronicling each feeling, all the highs and lows, a roller coaster of emotions. Even at the end, he said, "I am surrounded by terror. . . . But I am trusting in you, O LORD" (Psalm 31:13–14 NLT). In spite of his paralyzing fear, he understood who God was, which gave him the courage to relinquish his fearful emotions to trust in God. David intimately knew God and understood God was always with him.

This is what you can do. In spite of your overwhelming feelings of fear and despair, you can turn to God and trust he is there with you. Notice, David did not say he waited until he *felt* like God was near. By faith alone, he trusted God was with him even though he still felt terrified.

Emotions can be intense, erratic, surprising, and overwhelming. They will ebb and flow. Like David, allow yourself to feel them. Find a place that is safe where you can express your true feelings uninhibited. You can write about them, talk about them, yell them, sing them, cry about them, lament over them. When you are alone, it doesn't matter how you express them; what matters is you acknowledge and validate them in a way that feels safe. However, when you are with other people, be careful not to use others as a sounding board for pent-up anger. Be sure to also refrain from ruminating by complaining, moaning, and groaning, as these things may only multiply your intense emotions.

FEELINGS: FACT OR FICTION

Your feelings can often trick you, paralyze you, and deceive you. Like Tori feeling tired. Her feelings tried to convince her she was doomed to have a bad day. When you acknowledge your feelings, you can then fact-check them. Ask yourself, *Does this feeling fit the current facts around the situation I am facing?* Just because you feel angry doesn't mean anger is warranted. Just because you feel hopeless doesn't mean it is hopeless. Just because I felt like the roller-coaster ride was never going to end did not mean it would last forever. Knowing the truth behind your feelings often helps you move beyond them.

Feelings can convince you into believing you will feel hopeless forever. This is especially true during times of tragedy and grief. Your emotions are so intense and overwhelming you cannot imagine feeling anything different. But your feelings are not good predictors of truth. They can be deceiving. When I was on Space Mountain, I thought the ride would never stop, but when I saw the light at the end of the tunnel, I was never more relieved because I realized the ride would soon be over. Your feelings will still ebb and flow, and you will still have days that are up and down—but having a means of self-expression is like having a safety belt hold you in and keep you safe when you are on the roller coaster of emotions.

Like my friend Miranda who lost her baby unexpectedly—out of nowhere, an onslaught of emotions hit and sent her reeling. This roller-coaster ride of emotional ups and downs felt like it would never go away. This terrifying experience is often what happens when you walk through a painful and devastating circumstance. You think you will never feel joy again, that you are doomed to be in this dark place forever. One day you feel intense anger; the next, depression; then you feel numb. There seems to be no predictor. You assume all you can do is grab on tight and hope it doesn't get worse. At the time you cannot see anything but darkness—you are holding on trying to stay in control—and your feelings trick you into thinking it will never end, but it isn't true. Even if you cannot see it, there is a light at the end of the tunnel. Thankfully, the roller-coaster ride of emotions will eventually come to an end.

The intensity of your emotions can take you under if you do not learn to recognize what thoughts precipitate your feelings. Training yourself to think differently is essential to getting off of the roller coaster of emotions. Staying off the roller coaster is a learning process; it will not be automatic, so be patient with yourself and show yourself some compassion. Engage in self-soothing activities. These calming actions will stop the acceleration of the roller coaster, giving you an exit to the ride. Once off the ride, radically accept where you are at the moment.

MANAGING THE INTENSITY OF YOUR EMOTIONS

While you are learning how to understand your emotional responses, it is important to manage the intensity of your feelings. Bringing down your emotional energy is essential, especially if it is so high you cannot think straight. To do this you can use different strategies to activate your senses in an effort to help you tolerate your distressing feelings. For example, you can use something as simple as temperature to distract your thoughts just long enough to break the emotional spiral. If you are feeling intense anger or fear, take a piece of ice in your hand and hold it as long as possible. This may seem a bit unorthodox, but the intensity of the cold you feel will distract your intrusive thoughts about how angry or fearful you are long enough to break the spiraling emotional weight of the feelings. It may be a little uncomfortable, but your mind will fixate on the cold sensation in your hand instead of ruminating on your emotional pain. Another approach to using cold temperature is taking a cool shower or splashing cold water onto your face. These are not permanent solutions, but they are simple techniques you can use in an effort to initially stop the emotional spinning.

If you are sad and grieving, try activating your senses with warm temperatures by drinking a cup of hot tea or coffee, curling up in a cozy blanket, or laying out in the sun. Using warmth can also help you self-soothe, which is an important tool when you are overcome with emotions. Try to activate all of your senses with something pleasant such as looking at beautiful scenery or family photos, listening to calming music or ocean waves, tasting something sweet or minty, feeling something soft or petting a dog, or smelling a nice candle or a favorite lotion. Calming your senses will help you relax and release tension while decreasing the impact of your emotions. You may also find it helpful to distract yourself with fun activities, chores, errands, or even your breathing to take an emotional break in your mind. All of these strategies are good for short-term relief and bringing down the intensity of overwhelming emotions that make you spin.

Once the spinning stops, you can then evaluate the triggering event to your emotional reaction. This is best done through journaling. Journal your thoughts, perceptions, feelings, and ideas about the precipitating event. This can eventually lead you to the root of your emotional reactions. Once the intensity of your emotions decreases, it is important to find ways to change your response to the emotional trigger.

Change is easier when your emotional intensity is lower. Being less emotionally charged allows you to have more mental space to make different choices. Having less intense feelings, however, does not mean you will not get stuck. Even though you may not be overtaken by your emotions, you can still get emotionally entangled. Being stuck and entangled in an undesirable emotional response is an indicator to you that you need to take intentional action to move forward.

There are methods to help you move ahead when you feel crippled by a particular emotion. These strategies are especially helpful with feelings of depression, sadness, grief, and anger. If you act in a way that is opposite to how you are feeling or what your emotions are telling you to do, you begin to change how you feel.

When you are feeling sad, act as though you are happy, maintaining an upbeat tone of voice and having an upright, open posture. Get active. Put on exciting music, dance in your room, do a lively workout, or go on a run. Do anything to get your body moving.

When you are feeling angry, ease back, take a time-out, and be kind to whoever you are angry with. Low-intensity emotions are easier to manage, especially with opposite action. Changing your behavior to do something opposite from the way you feel will eventually change your perceptions, causing you to experience an emotional shift. Once this change occurs, your mind is free to look deeper into what initially triggered you to have that particular emotional reaction.

SMOKE FROM A DIFFERENT FIRE

Having an emotional response can sometimes be perplexing and confusing, especially when the reaction seems out of range given the precipitating event. You wonder, *Why did I get so angry and frustrated over something so small or insignificant?* Initially, your reaction seems warranted, but suddenly, like a bicycle going downhill gaining speed without pedaling, your emotions accelerate without you intentionally meaning to react with such intensity. Like gravity pulling the bike downhill, your reaction is automatic and inevitable. I call this uncontrolled reaction "smoke from a different fire."

Think about it like this: You walk outside your tent while camping, and off in the distance you see smoke. You assume it is coming from a neighboring campfire—a safe assumption—but upon further inspection you learn it is smoke from a forest fire. Likewise, your emotions can be the result of something you think is contained and obvious, but they actually originate from something different—something deeper, dark, hidden—something with the potential to cause damage. When you have smoke from a different fire, your reaction may seem out of range given the circumstance. There is something deep-seated, something bigger, more sinister behind the reaction. When you do not give your feelings a voice, they sit in wait, simmering below the surface. Then, out of nowhere, they unexpectedly boil over.

This sudden, explosive reaction happens in marriages a lot. Your reactions to situations seem overcharged. For example, you can be extremely upset that your spouse comes home from working all day and walks straight into his office without acknowledging you. So one day you let him have it, and he is caught completely off guard, not knowing this ritual triggers an emotional war zone for you. What is really upsetting you isn't just about his behavior at the moment; rather it's about buried feelings of neglect within your relationship. These feelings of neglect are the culprit of the billowing smoke; you easily mistake them for another fire.

Rather than talk about these feelings, you conceal them and put them on the back burner. Each time he walks into his office without acknowledging you, his actions reinforce your sense of rejection, which causes your emotions to boil over. When you get to your emotional boiling point, you overreact. Your reaction is no longer isolated to him going into his office; rather it is all of your feelings rooted in rejection and emotional neglect within your marriage. Failure to acknowledge these feelings creates a smoky fire that can be mistaken for something else, like the immediate reaction of your spouse neglecting to greet you when he arrives home. Over time, this smoke can become deadly.

This behavior is not limited to marriages; it can happen in any relationship. For example, your friend is late for lunch, and you get overly upset. You fear she was late because you were not important enough. Your feelings are entrenched in shame. You feel unimportant and unappreciated and fear being alone. These feelings are rooted in abandonment issues from past losses you have encountered; they are not directly related to your friend being late to lunch. Nor does your friend devalue you and your time—she simply did not allow enough margin to factor in unexpected traffic. However, knowing she was caught in traffic does not stop you from overreacting. This is smoke from a different fire. It has been simmering over time, making you overly fearful of being rejected or abandoned.

When you encounter unexpected loss, like my friend Miranda, who suddenly lost her baby the day she gave birth, your emotions initially spill out everywhere. Often as the days slip by, you learn to bury them, numbing yourself of the immediate pain. This seems like a viable solution, because feeling numb is better than feeling pain. But refusing to give your feelings a voice and denying your awareness of them allows them to simmer. These feelings will eventually show up, sometimes with a vengeance. Your unattended feelings and emotions will deeply root themselves into the core of who you are, creating a fortress around you and keeping those closest to you at arm's length. These feelings are at bay for a while, but eventually they will burst into a sudden blaze of smoke and fire, potentially destroying those in its path.

No matter how dark, intense, and ugly your feelings are, understanding and acknowledging them will help you accept the truth about how you really feel. Discovering the root of your feelings will move you forward in the healing process. Expressing your feelings and safely getting them out into the open when you are alone and reflective keeps you from going inward and hiding. It keeps you from exposing your emotions in ways you did not intend. When you bury your feelings, they surface unexpectedly, often in full force, leaving you blindsided. When you don't notice and attend to your feelings, they get expressed through the back door like smoke from a different fire. This is when "out of nowhere" your feelings show up when you least expect it.

But if you follow David's example and create an outlet for your feelings to be acknowledged and expressed in a productive way, you can prevent an unexpected emotional expression of smoke and fire. Sitting in the awareness of your emotions allows you to become the master of your feelings and gain control of your reactions to emotionally charged situations. There are occasions, however, where you feel so out of control and depressed you are not sure how to get to the root. Finding the root can be elusive. It can feel like grabbing your shadow. Every time you reach out to touch the gray image of yourself, you end up empty-handed. Not having a clear path to find the root to your emotional responses can seem discouraging, but don't be disheartened. Keep looking. Ask yourself what you think could be the root cause and journal, talk to a friend, or share with a counselor about your opinions and pray. Ask God to help you find the root.

HIJACKED BY YOUR EMOTIONS

Many times our emotions take over hijacking our rationale. These emotional outbursts or crushing emotions of despair are what control our lives. We are unable to respond to life—we are only able to react. Our emotions hijack our ability to manage the intensity of our feelings in a healthy and productive way. When we are emotionally hijacked, we are left to pick up the pieces of the aftermath.

Your feelings become so overwhelming you have difficulty completing the tasks that are expected of you. Thoughts of getting out of bed, getting dressed, and doing all that is expected seem too much at times. The cup of sorrow feels too bitter to swallow. You feel more guilt and shame for feeling this way, but it doesn't change your feelings of sadness. Some days you manage, but others you do not. The hopelessness is too great, the despair too deep. You stay home in bed with covers over your head and you sleep.

Or perhaps you're the person on the other end of the spectrum. You keep yourself busy enough to never stop, never be still, and never think. This is how you keep the despair at bay. You shut everyone out. You don't talk about it, don't think about it; you just run away, hide, and pretend it's not there. But sitting in the shadows are your deep-seated emotions, waiting to erupt. When they do, the intensity of such a rush of emotion is not warranted.

Whichever person you are, this is what it looks like to be hijacked by your emotions and to have your feelings turn against you.

There is a term we use in therapy called *complicated grief.* This is when a person moves beyond the normal grieving process and gets stuck in their sorrow and despair. They fail to move through their pain into a place where they can't accept loss in their life. When you experience complicated grief, your feelings of pain and sorrow are so debilitating that you have an inability to resume your life with any sense of resolve and closure. The hurt and anguish are so great that it can transcend any attempt to find resolution, leaving you stuck in your heartache.

So many individuals find themselves in this very spot where they feel stuck. It may even be you. If you are in the depths of your sorrow and cannot seem to find your way out, there is hope. Even though all of our feelings are valid, they are not good predictors of reality. They are not necessarily tellers of truth. This is good news. Because feelings are so persuasive, you can easily allow them to hijack you, stealing your ability to move beyond them. Feelings can be deceptive, and because of this deception, you cannot depend on them to accurately navigate you through crises. It is important, even vital, to embrace your feelings, but you cannot always act on your emotional urges.

When your sadness overwhelms you, this emotion may be signaling to you to retreat and isolate and ruminate on your feelings, but this is not a productive and effective way to live. These emotions will hijack you into behaving in a way that only increases and perpetuates your pain. If you are stuck in this pattern, it is important to bring the intensity of your emotions down and practice doing the opposite of what your emotions tell you to do.

Your feelings help you understand your behavior, your reactions, and your brokenness. They can give you signals about the environment around you, but they do not always tell you the truth. Just because you feel a certain way does not mean it is true. For example, Miranda struggled with feelings of guilt, thinking she could have done something to prevent the sudden death of her baby, when in reality she had done everything "right." *Feeling guilty doesn't make you guilty.*

When I was riding Space Mountain, I felt anxious every time the roller coaster jolted me into an upward climb. Overcome with fear, I thought at any second the ride was going to make a sudden drop downward and I would be in danger. Trusting these feelings led me to experience an overwhelming amount of dread and apprehension. My feelings were trying to convince me I was going to take a sudden drop at any second. My anxiety was not based on truth.

In reality, the ride often took a turn instead of dropping me downward. More importantly, the ride would not be allowed to operate if it was unsafe. Rather than increasing my angst, the turn brought relief. The turn changed my perception, showing me that my feelings were not true.

SPIRALING THOUGHTS

It was not my feelings alone that created my anxiety—it was also my thoughts. My thoughts caused my feelings of anxiety to overwhelm and consume me. It was reasonable for me to feel somewhat anxious while on the ride, but unreasonable for the feelings of anxiety to overtake me with paralyzing fear.

The same is true in life. Some feelings are warranted given the situation you are experiencing, but the degree to which you experience these feelings are a direct result of your thoughts. Your thoughts play an important role in how you feel, as your feelings also play a role in how you are thinking; the two are tightly woven together. When your thoughts begin to spiral and you begin to ruminate, your emotional intensity increases, and your feelings of anguish multiply. Changing this interaction between thoughts and feelings is vital to staying on course and achieving true emotional freedom.

Because your feelings can distort your perception of reality through faulty thinking, the cycle of your perceptions, thoughts, and feelings loop faster and faster to the point of your feelings becoming unmanageable. Your feelings try to convince you they are the source of truth, becoming the captain of the ship steering your further and further away from reality. Adopting this altered perception can cause your feelings to derail your thoughts. Your feelings can convince you life is hopeless, or you are a bad person. Your feelings have a way of searching out evidence to justify feeling a particular way. You might look at your circumstances and tell yourself life is too hard, too painful to go on, so you have no choice but to remain stuck in your pain. You find yourself thinking, *If I hadn't done* this, *then* that *wouldn't have happened.* If you rely on your feelings for truth, you will end up hijacked and stuck.

Expressing your feelings in a productive way must come with an understanding that they may not be based on truth. This understanding can help you accept your feelings just as they are. They do not have to be based on certainty of fact for you to acknowledge and validate them. Remember, feelings are not good or bad; they just are. The initial goal in managing how you feel is to bring the intensity down to a level where you can think clearly, go opposite of your emotion, and be mindful of your urges to behave in a destructive way. This will prevent you from overreacting and causing more emotional or relational damage. In time, you will learn how to weigh your emotions against the truth, allowing you the freedom to change your patterns of thinking so you can complete the process of rewiring your brain.

I can't say it enough. Even though feelings may not be predictors of truth, it is important for you to acknowledge and become present with them so you can understand why you feel the way you do. When you find yourself feeling as though you are in a dark pit, thinking your life is too hard and too painful, your feelings begin to suffocate you. In this dark place, you are held captive by your emotional turmoil, and you become defeated by your own will—the will to give up, to give in. This period of emotional intensity and hopelessness is the moment you need to embrace, affirm, and bring your feelings into your full awareness and then let go of them.

It may seem counterproductive to validate such hopeless feelings, but this validation works like a rubber band. When you pull against a rubber band, the tension increases. The more you pull, the tighter the tension becomes; but when you let go suddenly, all of the tension is gone. Validating and understanding the way you feel is like letting go of the rubber band. Once you embrace and attend to those unwanted feelings, the tension stops, and the cycle of rumination has been broken. You have permission to take everything in and drink your cup of sorrow with the hope your life will be worth living once again.

If accepting your feelings seems impossible right now, understand fear is often the motivating factor that keeps you from embracing your pain and then letting it go. Fear drives you to run from your feelings or to bury them—fear of pain, fear of truth, fear of guilt, fear of shame. You fear that if you sit with your emotions, they will overcome you. They will be too much, too overwhelming to the point of taking you under. Living with the tension of unwanted feelings can be suffocating. The more you resist and run away from the way you feel, the tighter the tension becomes. Pushing your feelings aside—or worse, succumbing to these feelings by letting them bring you into a false reality and tell you lies about yourself and the world around you—will hijack your life with hopelessness and despair. You will feel stuck and convinced there is no way out, no relief, no resolution. Holding on to painful emotions will keep you trapped in a pit—the dark pit of despair and hopelessness.

But releasing them will bring you relief. Letting go is a gradual process. Realize moving forward doesn't occur in giant steps. The steps are usually small, moving you forward bit by bit. As time passes you will see how far you have moved.

LETTING GO

Sometimes you cling so tightly to these intense feelings because they are familiar to you. Somehow your unpleasant feelings actually feel safe. What happens when you let go? It's scary at first, stepping away from the familiar, but it is necessary for your emotional freedom. Holding on to your feelings so tightly without the willingness to let go will keep you from moving forward.

It may feel safe to continue in your grief or in your pain because you have become accustomed and dearly acquainted with these feelings. It may even feel scary to open up to the possibility of being free from these emotions because, in a strange way, the familiarity of them is comforting. Does letting go mean you no longer care about what has passed? Perhaps you are afraid that letting go of your feelings means letting go of your loss. You think holding on to your emotions helps you hold on to what has been taken from you.

Letting go of your sorrow is not done all at once. It is done piece by piece. Holding on to your emotional pain fools you into thinking you are being loyal and that letting go of them makes you disloyal. When you understand these emotions are more about familiarity than they are about loyalty, you will be better equipped to walk in them and then move past them. Letting go doesn't mean you are walking away from your memories—it simply means you allow yourself to detangle the sorrow and regret from your past and allow your memories to be a means of comfort and connection or serve as a reminder of your forgiveness and resolution. As you loosen the grip on your feelings, you will be able to let go of the familiar and find a sense of relief and hope.

To let go, you must allow your feelings to come and go, like waves in the ocean. When the intense wave of sadness or anxiety arises, you have to embrace them and attend to them. Then, when those feelings subside, you must allow yourself to feel joy without letting fear or shame hijack your positive feelings. When you let go of painful emotions of sorrow, fear, loneliness, rejection, guilt, and shame, you unlock the prison walls you've built to numb yourself and you set yourself free from the captivity of intense feelings. You begin to say yes to bearing the full weight of your feelings, and no to grabbing hold of them for dear life or pushing them as far away from you as possible. You come into full awareness of each emotion, noticing which emotions you are experiencing, and let go of them as you express, validate, and do the opposite of what your feelings tell you to do.

The first step in working through and letting go of your feelings is to own them. By acknowledging your feelings, whether warranted or not, you validate your pain, your grief, and your sorrow. This is an important step in taking control of your emotional well-being. There is a familiar saying, "You can't change what you don't acknowledge." This is especially true with your feelings. Your feelings will not change if you cannot admit to having them. To prevent them from hijacking your life, you have to first embrace and acknowledge them, identifying which emotions you are experiencing. It is helpful to validate your emotions as well, encouraging yourself with statements such as, "It makes sense given my situation that I would feel this way," or "No wonder I am feeling this way given my past experiences." In addition, you can validate yourself by saying, "All actions have consequences, and everything has a cause, so everything has led up to exactly where I am," or "Anyone would feel this way based on what has happened." These statements help you believe that your feelings are not bad or that you are not crazy for feeling the way you feel and acting a certain way.

Your emotions and feelings are like an unexpected relative who arrives at your front door. Though they may be unwelcome at first, you must come to accept your feelings and let them in for a stay at your home. They won't be there forever, but if you don't let them in, they will keep incessantly knocking at your door. Similarly, you must let your feelings come into your full awareness, have a stay in your mind, and let them leave when it's time for them to go.

FOLLOW DAVID'S LEAD

Key to David's survival was being able to encounter and express the beauty and nature of God alongside his feelings of heartbreak and shame. It kept him moving ahead, believing God would always be by his side and giving him all he needed to overcome his pain. This is why David never got stuck. Tripped and stumbled, yes, but taken out? Never. He always kept moving regardless of the situation he was facing.

Often when David was grieving, he would write a psalm. On one occasion he wrote: "Be merciful to me, LORD, for I am in distress; my eyes grow weak with sorrow, my soul and body with grief. My life is consumed by anguish" (Psalm 31:9–10).

It is clear from reading these verses David was suffering. We are not certain of the incident that occurred in his life that precipitated these words, but we are convinced of his overwhelming pain. Perhaps he wrote this while on the run from Saul or when his son, his own flesh and blood, Absalom, came back into his hometown to kill him. Whatever the case, David was in distress, and he coped by writing about his feelings, reaching out to God, and asking him for deliverance.

David opened Psalm 31 by asking God to be his refuge. "In you, LORD, I have taken refuge; let me never be put to shame; deliver me in your righteousness. Turn your ear to me, come quickly to my rescue; be my rock of refuge, a strong fortress to save me. Since you are my rock and my fortress, for the sake of your name lead and guide me" (vv. 1–3). David knew his hope and emotional refuge would come from God and God alone. He could not trust his circumstances or his feelings, but he could trust God to be his redeemer.

David also wrote in Psalm 91, "He who dwells in the shelter of the Most High will abide in the shadow of the Almighty. I will say to the LORD, 'My refuge and my fortress, my God, in whom I trust'" (vv. 1–2 ESV). How comforting to know we can rest in the shadow of the Almighty. We can find a respite from our anguish and our suffering when we simply run to the Father and allow him to become our stronghold, our defense, our place of safety.

When we enter his presence in prayer and cry out to God, Christ defends our needs and protects us from thoughts Satan uses to intimidate us into believing life will never feel good again. Christ places a barrier around our minds, keeping emotions that want to take us out at bay.

God was David's go-to. He knew being in the presence of God was his safe place when he felt defeated. God was the source of his strength, which gave him the courage to take another step—to keep moving.

In Psalm 143:1–8, he penned these words:

LORD, hear my prayer, listen to my cry for mercy; in your faithfulness and righteousness come to my relief. Do not bring your servant into judgment, for no one living is righteous before you. The enemy pursues me, he crushes me to the ground; he makes me dwell in the darkness like those long dead. So my spirit grows faint within me; my heart within me is dismayed. I remember the days of long ago; I meditate on all your works and consider what your hands have done. I spread out my hands to you; I thirst for you like a parched land. Answer me quickly, LORD; my spirit fails. Do not hide your face from me or I will be like those who go down to the pit. Let the morning bring me word of your unfailing love, for I have put my trust in you. Show me the way I should go, for to you I entrust my life.

As you read his words you can feel his heartbreak and experience his agony. He sounds crushed and devastated. He is pouring out the depths of his soul to God, knowing God is the one who is going to get him through his desperation. It is clear to us in reading these passages that David trusted God to reach out and save him from his despair. He did not hesitate for a second to tell God exactly how he was feeling, because he knew God would still love him in spite of his intense emotions. God was David's safe place to land, his friend, his refuge, his Savior. Embracing his feelings, expressing them, and trusting God to deliver him is why David did not become trapped in his own fear and sorrow. This is why he was able to keep moving forward in his grief.

I have been blessed with three wonderful children. When they were small, they would often fall down and hurt themselves. Every time this would happen, they would always run directly into my arms so I could make them feel better. Sometimes all they had to do was call my name and I would come to them. When they were hurting, I was there.

My youngest loved for me to scoop her up and kiss her scrapes and bruises. She wanted me to cuddle her and tell her over and over how much I loved her while I ran my fingers through her long blonde hair.

She was always drumming up some kind of injury just so she could stop me from whatever I was doing and get me to love on her. She is now nineteen and still loves to reach out for a hug and an embrace to receive comfort, validation, and the assurance that her pain will not last forever.

My children needed me to help them move past their moment of injury and pain to find a place of comfort and reassurance that everything was going to be okay.

Entering the presence of God during times of sorrow is like my daughter climbing into my lap to be held when she was hurting. The warmth of my arms made her pain fade away. Because she understood my lap was a safe place, she knew my touch would always make things better.

The same is true with you and Christ. When you come into his presence, he will provide a safe place where his touch will give you peace amid your pain and sorrow. He will validate your feelings just as he did David's.

When you grieve, God can and will place you under the shadow of his wings, allowing you to feel heartbreak while comforting you during the process. This is because he gives you hope to believe your pain will not last forever and your life will move forward in a positive way. In Isaiah 61:1, the prophet Isaiah tells us Christ came to bring good news to the poor, to bind up the brokenhearted, to proclaim freedom for the captives, and release from darkness for the prisoners.

Isn't that what you feel like when you are suffering from grief—like a brokenhearted child and a hopeless prisoner? Like David, your eyes have grown weak with sorrow, and you need to find refuge in the shelter of the Most High.

You are assured in this passage that Christ has come to bind up your broken heart and set you free from darkness. Take David's lead and cry out to God and allow Christ to bind up your broken heart.

The good news is God does not wait for you to resolve your grief before he intervenes. He will do for you what he did for David. He will listen to your heartache with a merciful heart, opening his arms to provide a refuge and fortress for your soul even when you are consumed with anger and bitterness. Often these are the exact emotions you experience during times of crises and grief, and they are warranted!

If you fail to embrace where you are and fail to admit it is not where you want to be, then you will remain stuck. But if you embrace your feelings and validate them, you will be one step closer to healing.

YOU ARE WHERE YOU NEED TO BE

Wherever you find yourself in your journey, you are where you need to be. Embrace where you are and what you're feeling. Do not be afraid to feel. Let your feelings tell you what you need to know and where you need to go next. Do what David did and share the depths of your heart with God. Do not hold back. David fully trusted God, which is why he was named a man after God's own heart. He was not afraid to be real with God, so real that God was able to touch David deeply. Why? Because David let God in deeply. He let him into the depths of his soul.

Embracing your feelings and truthfully acknowledging your emotions is an important step in moving forward in your journey. Although they can be intense, overwhelming, erratic, even deceptive, they can also be liberating, comforting, and purposeful. Feelings are what make you human. They set you apart. Being able to understand them and learn how to tame them are what separates you from all other living creatures. It is time to stop running away and hiding. Open your arms and find refuge in the shadow of the Most High, and he will give you comfort as you hold your cup of sorrow.

HELPFUL TOOLS

1. Remember your emotions are not good or bad. They just are. Your emotions can give insight into your thoughts, beliefs, and behaviors.
2. Name your emotion. What emotion are you experiencing right now (i.e., anger, sadness, fear, or shame)?
3. Identify the intensity and validity of your emotion. Does your emotion and its intensity fit the current facts of the situation? If your emotion is too intense to move forward, try self-soothing or using temperature to bring down the intensity. If your emotion or its intensity does not "fit the facts," try an opposite action or distract yourself with activities.
4. Feelings do not always tell the truth. Just because you feel a certain way does not mean it is true. Notice when your emotions become ineffective and get in the way of moving forward. Try methods to bring down the emotional intensity or go opposite to the emotion.
5. Identify the root behind your emotions: Acknowledge your emotions may be smoke from a different fire. Challenge your negative thoughts and beliefs that are making you feel bad or causing you to overreact.
6. Be mindful of your emotions and bring them into your full awareness. Notice your emotions and their intensity coming and going as waves.
7. Validate your emotions with encouraging self-talk and embrace where you are.
8. Remember that letting go of your feelings is not done all at once. It happens gradually.

7

A Cup of Freedom

Understanding Your Body, Soul, and Spirit

*I*n my early twenties, I decided to enter graduate school to become a marriage and family therapist. I graduated from the University of North Texas with a master of education in marriage and family counseling. The following year I passed the state exam for professional counselors and began working in private practice as an LPC (licensed professional counselor) for many years.

When I was in my mid-teens, I felt God had called me into ministry to work with women, so becoming a therapist seemed like the right path for me. I worked with women who struggled with depression, anxiety, and past trauma. I not only believed I had the skills from the training I received in graduate school, but also thought I could relate to their experiences, given the amount of childhood trauma I had encountered personally. Working with emotionally wounded women with broken spirits allowed me to fulfill the calling I believed God had placed on my heart for a season.

I eventually married and had three children. After having my children, I decided to stay at home with them—that is, until my husband asked me to help him manage his medical practice. When my two oldest children were in elementary school, we moved to the small town of Bastrop, Texas, where Jeff, my husband, opened a private OB/GYN practice. It was an ideal place for him to work and for us to raise a family. I worked part-time to help him get the practice established. After a few years, we decided that having doctors conveniently provide health care to the rural communities was a much-needed service in obstetrics, so we decided to open another office in a small town nearby. We eventually opened five offices in several surrounding rural communities and towns in the Austin area.

Rather than working as an LPC, I used my counseling skills and knowledge to manage these offices. I spent a great deal of my time working with our employees to help them gain better communication skills and problem-solving strategies. After working to build this medical practice for seventeen years, my husband and I decided to make a change. He no longer wanted the responsibility of the practice management and just wanted to see patients within a hospital setting. As for me, I was not sure what I wanted to do. I knew I was exhausted mentally and emotionally from managing our offices in today's complicated medical climate. I was at a crossroads. Although I had worked as a therapist, I often wondered why the door for me to work directly in ministry with women never opened. Had I been given that chance, I would have done it, but it was clear God had placed me on another path. When we sold the practice, I felt lost. My two oldest children were successfully launched and out of our home. My youngest was a junior in high school.

After managing a demanding practice and walking through many unexpected and painful storms during the previous twenty years, I felt depleted and hollow inside. The thought of sitting quietly at home with no demands sounded quite appealing. I wondered if I still had the gifts God had given me and if I could even use them after so many years had passed. I felt as though I was in a small boat drifting along an isolated and lonely shore, uncertain whether to keep going or take the boat onto dry ground and get off for good.

Out of the blue, one of my oldest and dearest friends called and asked me if I would come to one of her worship nights in Dallas. I had met

Rachelle while on a mission trip to London when I was sixteen years old. We immediately connected and developed a close bond and deep friendship. We were roommates in college and remained close after we graduated and married. However, we drifted apart when I moved to the Greater Austin area. When she called, it was as if no time had passed between us. We quickly caught up and were connected once again. Not having much on my plate, I agreed to go to the worship night. I showed up early to help her set up for the event. It was great being with her again. I was looking forward to an evening of worship but not expecting anything out of the ordinary to happen.

I usually sit in the front row when I attend events. It helps me stay focused. I walked in, set my belongings down in the front of the auditorium, and waited for Rachelle to begin the service. As she led us in the first song, I felt a tug in my heart to move to the back row and minister to a lady sitting alone. Not wanting to move, I contemplated ignoring this feeling. I knew if I sat in the back of the room, I would be distracted by all the movement in the building. After a few minutes of arguing with myself, I could not shake the feeling, so I picked up my things, walked to the back row, and stood beside the woman who was alone, not realizing God had a bigger plan.

God knows me well. Since I am an introvert, he knew I would not have had the courage to respond to an invitation to stand up and receive inner healing during a worship service had I been on the front row. He strategically moved me to the back of the room. Yes, I was able to pray with and minister to the lady standing next to me, but God wanted more. He wanted to restore my worn-out and weakened soul and revive the calling in my heart to minister to the brokenhearted. I came to that worship service hurting and lost. I had no idea what I was going to do in my life moving forward. I was tired and discouraged. Honestly, I did not believe I had any more to give. Rachelle started singing a song that talked about God making me into a vessel, and out of the crushing and the pressing, he would make new wine. I began to cry, feeling as though she was singing directly to me. When she extended an invitation to those who were hurting and wanted inner healing to stand and receive a touch from God, I knew God wanted me to respond. Moving me to the back row was God's way of saying, *I will meet you where you are.* If I had not moved back there, I would not have stood up. I would have missed out on the freedom and inner healing God wanted to give to me.

During that worship service, I felt like God was saying now was the time for me to minister directly to women, but I had no idea how that would happen. After the night of worship, I went back home and held on to this calling I felt in my heart. I spent my time resting, praying, and patiently waiting for God to open a door. A few months later, I was asked to become the director of women's ministry at a new campus church being launched later that year. I cried when I was asked to lead the women of this community, knowing the calling God had placed on my heart years ago as a teenager was now coming to pass.

While I was waiting, God set me free from the brokenness I had encountered over the years. This path to freedom began that night at worship when God started transforming my heart and mind and healing my weary and wounded soul. My spirit woke up and heard God calling me to him in a brand-new way.

BODY, SOUL, AND SPIRIT

Everyone has seasons of sorrow and brokenness. Some can move through these seasons easier than others. Have you ever been or are you currently in a season where you can't seem to move through your grief, heartache, or hopelessness? Maybe you feel like I did that night of the worship service, feeling as though you are drifting in a small boat along a lonely shore, uncertain of where you are going. You wonder if you should just dock your boat and get off. God can and will bring you emotional and spiritual freedom, but it is up to you to reach out and receive it.

Your core beliefs, thoughts, feelings, and perceptions all profoundly impact your emotional and spiritual well-being. Your natural man and spiritual man are not separate. They work together in tandem or against each other at war. To walk in wholeness and healing, it is essential to understand how your body, soul, and spirit can work together with your thoughts, feelings, and behaviors to achieve spiritual and emotional freedom.

In 1 Thessalonians 5:23, Paul wrote, "Now may the God of peace himself sanctify you completely, and may your whole spirit and soul and body be kept blameless at the coming of our Lord Jesus Christ" (ESV). Hebrews 4:12 says, "For the word of God is living and active, sharper than any two-edged sword, piercing to the division of soul and of spirit, of joints and of marrow, and discerning the thoughts and intentions of the heart" (ESV). These two verses clearly show we all have a body, a soul, and a spirit, each serving a different purpose.

Our body literally refers to our flesh, organs, joints, and marrow. In the Bible, our body is called the temple. "Or do you not know that your body is a temple of the Holy Spirit within you, whom you have from God? You are not your own, for you were bought with a price. So glorify God in your body" (1 Corinthians 6:19–20 ESV). In the Old Testament, the temple was the place where the children of Israel worshiped, but within that temple, there existed a sacred room called the Holy of Holies, the place inhabited by God.

Like the Holy of Holies, our spirit is God's dwelling place—the place where God lives and sin cannot dwell. The Holy of Holies was the innermost room that housed the ark of the covenant. Only the sanctified high priest was allowed in this room. This sacred chamber was the place where the high priest atoned for the sins of the people. It was so holy that anyone other than the priest would die upon entry. God dwelled in this sacred place; therefore, no sin could enter in, and if it did, death was imminent. Understanding the idea that no sin could enter into the Holy of Holies is essential. God is without sin and cannot exist where sin resides. This truth is how we know God lives in our spirit, not in our flesh or in our soul. Your soul is the dwelling place of your mind, free will, and heart. The soul is where sin can abide. Because of the sin in your soul, God cannot live there. In the Bible, the soul is often referred to as the flesh: "But I say, walk by the Spirit, and you will not gratify the desires of the flesh" (Galatians 5:16 ESV). The "desires of the flesh" refers to the desires of the soul, which is sin. This sin within your soul influences your mind, free will, and heart.

- Your mind is the center of operations; it houses your thoughts, beliefs, and perceptions.
- Your free will is the mechanism by which you make all of your decisions.
- Your heart encompasses your emotions and feelings.

Satan knows that where he has the most influence is in your mind. He will distort, manipulate, falsify, and exaggerate the truth to create a stronghold within your core beliefs. These strongholds influence your free will. Your free will is activated and has to choose what to believe whenever lies and false beliefs taint your perception. When your mind is full of lies and distorted ideas about the things that are happening around you or to you, you can become discouraged, even tempted to sin. This discouragement can rob you of your faith and hope in God's ability to intervene on your behalf. You lose sight of where it is you need to go. Your free will takes over, and you find yourself questioning God and his plan for your life. When you choose to accept these lies and make decisions based on them, your feelings will be influenced by this distorted version of the truth prompting the way you behave. This cycle of thoughts, feelings, and behaviors directly results from your free will. Satan cannot make you choose your beliefs, nor will God make you believe a certain way. No, your free will decides what you will believe and how you will feel and behave. These choices initiate and influence your feelings, and your feelings are what elicit your behaviors.

Take the night when I attended that worship service, for example. I had started to believe a lie. Satan was planting ideas and thoughts into my head about my worth and plans for my future. He was trying to convince me I had done all I needed to do and had nothing else to give to others. I had the choice to believe this lie or not. I must confess, I spent more time than I would like to admit wanting to believe what Satan was peddling to me was the truth. I was tempted to give up. A big part of me wanted to walk away from any calling God had placed in my life and just be content with doing nothing of any great importance or significance.

But that night, I pushed those thoughts out of my head. I chose to believe God wanted me to minister to that woman sitting in the back of the room, so I surrendered to the prompting of the Holy Spirit by changing seats and praying for this woman even though I did not feel like it. I decided myself to move to the back of the room. God did not make me move, nor did Satan convince me to stay. Out of my free will,

I decided! This choice to surrender to the Holy Spirit by moving to the back row set my spiritual and emotional path to healing in motion.

You are in a battleground within your soul—your mind, your free will, and your heart. When you become a believer in Christ, God enters your spirit and resides there. Remember, your spirit represents the Holy of Holies, the place without sin. Because of sin, your spirit and soul often war against each other. Ephesians 6:12 explains, "For our struggle is not against flesh and blood, but against the rulers, against the authorities, against the powers of this dark world and against the spiritual forces of evil in the heavenly realms." This passage teaches us that there is an unseen battle that exists within the heavenly realms unforeseen by the human eye. This battle involves a real enemy—Satan. He has no authority over you as a Christian, but he does have access to your soul. Satan tries to influence you by inserting thoughts, perceptions, and core beliefs into your mind; impacting your heart (your feelings); and driving your behaviors (your free will).

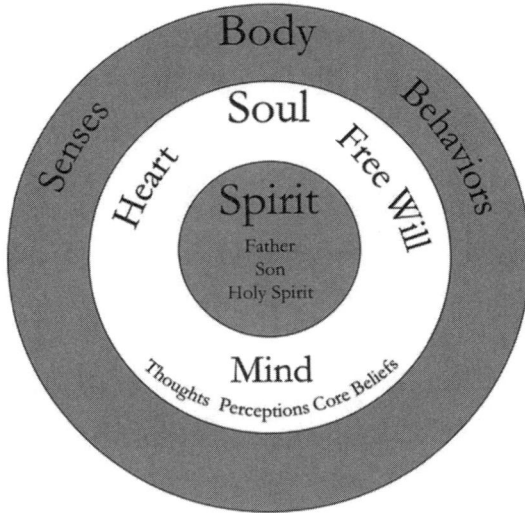

Whenever you feel discouraged and ask God to help you, a battle incites in the heavenly realms that you have to fight. Ephesians 6:11, 13–18 explains:

> Put on the full armor of God so that you can take your stand against the devil's schemes. . . . Therefore put on the full armor of God, so that when the day of evil comes, you may be able to stand your ground, and after you have done everything, to stand. Stand firm then, with the belt of truth buckled around your waist, with the breastplate of righteousness in place, and with your feet fitted with the readiness that comes from the gospel of peace. In addition to all this, take up the shield of faith, with which you can extinguish all the flaming arrows of the evil one. Take the helmet of salvation and the sword of the Spirit, which is the word of God. And pray in the Spirit on all occasions.

There is a spiritual battle that you must be prepared to fight as a believer in Christ. Satan tries to discourage you by throwing darts of fear, doubt, shame, worry, and disappointment into your mind, so putting on this armor in its entirety will prepare you for a battle that wars in the heavenly places as well as in your mind.

As a Christ-follower, you have to protect your mind. The mind is the point of entry for Satan. If you are a believer in Christ, he cannot enter your spirit, nor can he possess your body; he does not have that much power. This lack of power is why Satan tries to use the influence he has by inserting lies into your mind. He wants to intimidate you with fear and shame by creating strongholds within your core beliefs that keep you stuck. You become stuck because your decisions and behaviors are dictated by these false core beliefs, negative thinking, and feelings of fear and hopelessness. Satan tries his best to influence your mind, heart, and free will through his lies.

Understanding how Satan influences and tries to control your thinking equips you with the ability to stand against his lies. When you stand firm in your faith, you can use the knowledge of God's Word to stamp out and eliminate Satan's warped version of the truth. Replacing Satan's lies with God's truth enables you to see your circumstances from a different perspective, giving you the strength and courage to move forward in healing. Your feelings of discouragement turn into feelings of hope. Why? Because your thoughts, perceptions, and beliefs are grounded in God's truth, not Satan's lies. Remember, your feelings directly result from your thinking, and when your thinking changes, your heart (feelings) will follow suit, persuading change to occur within your free will (behavior). Wearing the full armor of God equips your soul for battle and will protect your mind and heart during the fight.

THE BATTLE OF THE SOUL AND THE SPIRIT

The truth of God's Word resides within your spirit. Because your spirit is the place where God dwells and is without sin, his truth cannot be tainted or distorted by Satan's lies. Your spirit is the Holy of Holies, the sacred place where sin cannot dwell. So the truth of God's Word that lives within your spirit cannot be manipulated or tarnished. However, because of sin, your soul has the ability to contaminate and pollute the truth of God's Word. God's truth will be distorted when you have a damaged filter lined with lies of the Enemy. These lies allow false core beliefs and strongholds to become deeply rooted within the core of your mind and heart, tainting your perception of the truth. This distortion of truth is because of Satan and sin. Although sin cannot reside within your spirit, it makes itself at home within your soul. Satan inserts himself into your mind, heart, and free will, persuading you to deny the truth and succumb to the Enemy's lies, often resulting in sin.

For example, if you have a filter lined with shame—beliefs that you are not good enough or are damaged goods—you may tell yourself you are disqualified, condemned, or judged by God's Word. Your shame will not allow you to accept God's grace and unconditional love that comes from receiving and embracing his truth. Being disqualified and unable to receive his unconditional redemptive love is not what the Word of God teaches us; rather, it is a distortion of God's Word by lies rooted in shame. These lies may say, *You are still a sinner and not worthy of God's grace. This verse does not apply to you. It only applies to those living the way they should be living. You have done too much to receive his grace. You will never be able to live a righteous life.*

These lies can drone on and on, convincing you God's Word is not valid for you. Satan knows the exact lie to keep you from receiving redemption and forgiveness amid your sinful living.

God does not ask you to make things right before you ask him into your heart. All he asks is for you to believe in him and surrender your heart. Knowing you are imperfect, he still promises to extend grace and help you despite your brokenness. Being unrighteous and getting it wrong is why we need his help.

As the office manager, I would tell our employees that they would not always get it right; they would inevitably make mistakes from time to time. I explained the importance of acknowledging their mistake and asking for help. The same is true for Christians. Christians are not always going to get it right. They will make mistakes. The important thing for Christians to understand is being willing to acknowledge their sin and ask God for help. Satan, however, wants to distort this truth and convince you that you are not worthy of God's love and forgiveness. He will try convincing you that the words written in the Bible are not for you.

Satan is an opportunist. When he sees you are vulnerable due to a difficult, challenging, or even tragic set of circumstances, he discretely tries to enter your soul, disguising himself as the truth. His goal is to move you as far away from the truth as he can with his crafty, cunning, and devious lies. Jesus described Satan as the master liar: "When he [Satan] lies, he speaks out of his own character, for he is a liar and the father of lies" (John 8:44 ESV). According to Peter in the Bible, Satan roams around like a contentious lion seeking to destroy the vulnerable. Peter warned us to "Be alert and of sober mind. Your enemy the devil prowls around like a roaring lion looking for someone to devour" (1 Peter 5:8).

For example, an individual facing an unexpected set of circumstances is tempted to think God does not care or is unwilling to heal their brokenness and grief. They find themself spinning in circles, trying to understand why. They ask how a loving God can allow this incident or tragedy even to happen. Satan sees their vulnerability and moves into action. He puts doubt into their mind about who God is and what he is willing to do. He tells them God doesn't care or is punishing them for something they have or have not done. The lies continue to mount. He tries to convince them to take matters into their own hands or turn away from a God who would allow such a terrible thing to happen. An offense and a root of bitterness are planted and will continue to grow. They grow like weeds in a garden without a gardener to pluck them out. Their thoughts, perceptions, and core beliefs are affected by Satan's lies on them. They struggle to know the truth. A battle within their mind ensues.

Your spirit houses the truth, but your free will within your soul decides whether it will receive or reject this truth. This decision results from the conflict you encounter within your spirit and soul—your mind, heart, and free will. Your spirit and soul are fighting against each other. Your spirit and flesh are at war to win over the allegiance of your free will by persuading you to surrender to either your spirit man or your soulish man. Surrendering to your spirit requires faith. Your free will has to choose to believe God is who he says he is despite your circumstances. You have to believe God's Word is absolute truth. Your flesh, however, often disregards God's truth. It lures you into focusing on what is in front of you—your pain, sorrow, and hopelessness. In Colossians 1:15–16, Paul explained the seen and unseen: "Christ is the visible image of the invisible God. He existed before anything was created and is supreme over all creation, for through him God created everything in the heavenly realms and on earth. He made the things we can see and the things we can't see—such as thrones, kingdoms, rulers, and authorities in the unseen world. Everything was created through him and for him" (NLT).

In this passage, Paul explained things are happening in the spiritual realm that we cannot see. God, in his sovereignty, is fighting on our behalf in the heavenlies. He tells us some things are clearly seen by our earthly eyes—the events surrounding our circumstances—but there are also things occurring in the supernatural that we cannot see. Our faith leads us to believe God is working on our behalf within the things that are not seen, but Satan wants to persuade us to look at our circumstances and use them to determine the truth about the nature and character of God. For example, if your experience does not point to the goodness of God, but instead to a cruel and unfair set of circumstances, you are more vulnerable to believing the lies Satan is telling you. These lies may cause you to doubt God or yourself. You may be tempted to fall into sin.

Paul provided for us his account of the struggle he encountered with his own battle over God's truth and sin within his own mind:

> So the trouble is not with the law, for it is spiritual and good. The trouble is with me, for I am all too human, a slave to sin. I don't really understand myself, for I want to do what is right, but I don't do it. Instead, I do what I hate. But if I know that what I am doing is wrong, this shows that I agree that the law is good. So I am not the one doing wrong; it is sin living in me that does it.
>
> And I know that nothing good lives in me, that is, in my sinful nature. I want to do what is right, but I can't. I want to do what is good, but I don't. I don't want to do what is wrong, but I do it anyway. But if I do what I don't want to do, I am not really the one doing wrong; it is sin living in me that does it.
>
> I have discovered this principle of life—that when I want to do what is right, I inevitably do what is wrong. I love God's law with all my heart. But there is another power within me that is at war with my mind. This power makes me a slave to the sin still within me. Oh, what a miserable person I am! Who will free me from this life that is dominated by sin and death? Thank God! The answer is in Jesus Christ our Lord. So you see how it is: In my mind I really want to obey God's law, but because of my sinful nature I am a slave to sin. (Romans 7:14–26 NLT)

This passage teaches us the importance of knowing and understanding God's Word (what Paul refers to as "the law"). Without it, you would not know what is right in the eyes of God. His Word is truth and can set you free when your free will chooses to live by God's truth and not by the desires of your flesh or sinful nature. Paul clearly demonstrated how your flesh and your spirit war against each other. Because of Satan's lies and the temptation to sin, your soulish or sinful man is at war with your spirit man. They are both trying to influence your free will to make a choice. A choice to walk in faith and believe in the unseen—to believe in what the Bible says about the goodness of God despite your circumstances. Or a choice to doubt God's Word and to believe in what is easily seen—your pain, sorrow, the unfortunate course of events, and the seeming lack of intervention by a "loving" God. Because of the battle warring against the truth and the lies in your soul—your mind, heart, and free will—this decision is not made without a fight.

You have to be prepared for this battle that occurs in your mind. You have to wear the spiritual armor discussed in Ephesians 6 to discern the Enemy's lies and to ward off the temptation to believe those lies. It is up to you to look for false core beliefs that initiate the cycle of thoughts, feelings, and behaviors within your mind, heart, and free will. Satan uses these false core beliefs to initiate the battle between your spirit and your soulish man. He creates strongholds in your mind to lead you down a path of disbelief and doubt. For example, Satan may try to convince you that you are not good enough and that God does not care about you. He knows that if he can persuade you into believing this lie, he can lead you farther and farther away from the truth. You must be spiritually alert to know it is Satan who is trying to convince you of this lie and get you to focus on the seen rather than the unseen. Your free will decides what to believe. You have to be prepared to fight. Wearing the full armor of God to protect you against the lies of the Enemy is essential to inner healing and emotional and spiritual freedom.

WALKING IN FREEDOM

Walking in freedom requires you to have the power to overcome strong-holds, false core beliefs, and fearful thinking. Simply knowing what the Bible says is not enough to overcome these obstacles. Why isn't the knowledge of God's Word enough? You would think just knowing the words written in the Bible would be sufficient to convince your free will to do what is right and to believe in the truth, but it is not. Knowledge by itself has no power source. Without power, they are just words. These words need a supernatural source to override the Enemy's lies that occur within your soul. It is like a light bulb. Without electricity, it is just a piece of glass unable to shed any light into the darkness, but the minute the light bulb is plugged in, it has the power to illuminate an entire room.

The Holy Spirit is the source of your power, which works like a light bulb. The Bible explains, "You will receive power when the Holy Spirit comes on you" (Acts 1:8). With the power that comes from the Holy Spirit, God's spoken Word, the Bible has the strength and intensity to override your negative thoughts and false core beliefs. However, without that power, the words often fall on deaf ears, meaning you cannot hear the truth. The truth is too hard to accept. It doesn't make sense in your mind. The way to walk in freedom is to access the power source of the Holy Spirit. This power will allow you to open the door of truth. Your spirit houses the undefiled truth of God's Word. To access this truth, you have to open the door to your spirit from your soul and choose to accept it.

So how does one open the door from their soul to their spirit? It is done by receiving God's unconditional love. Being saved and receiving unconditional love is the key to unlocking the door from your spirit to your soul. Without Jesus and without love, you do not have access to his power source. Because of sin and the accuser of your sin, Satan tries to convince you that you are unworthy and unable to receive God's mercy and saving grace. This belief is a lie! The Bible declares you cannot earn your salvation: "For by grace you have been saved through faith. And this is not your own doing; it is the gift of God, not a result of works, so that no one may boast" (Ephesians 2:8–9 ESV). Salvation is a gift given to you because of God's unconditional love and grace that has been extended to you. Romans 5:8 explains, "God shows his love for us in that while we were still sinners, Christ died for us" (ESV). Satan, however, wants to distort this truth by convincing you that you are unworthy. If he can make you believe you do not deserve God's saving grace and unconditional love, the door to receiving the pure, unblemished truth of God's Word remains locked. As a result, God's truth becomes tainted by your damaged filter lined with lies from Satan.

Your free will chooses to believe or not to believe the truth about your ability to accept and receive salvation and God's unconditional love. When you choose to believe you are worthy of salvation and surrender your heart to God, he enters your spirit, the Holy of Holies, the place without sin, and activates the power of the Holy Spirit to open the door for you to receive the truth of his Word.

Once this door has been opened, the Holy Spirit releases his power to supernaturally enable your mind, heart, and free will to receive the truth. You are given the ability to merge the knowledge of God's Word and the truth of God's Word together. Joining the knowledge in your mind with the truth in your spirit cannot be done without the power that comes from the Holy Spirit. Without the power of the Holy Spirit, you are like the light bulb that has not been connected to its power source. This lack of supernatural power is why the knowledge of God's Word is not enough to change the way you think or believe. To convince your free will to have faith, you must access your power source—the Holy Spirit.

When this merger occurs, the truth of his Word is revealed through the power of the Holy Spirit. This revelation of God's spoken Word is called the Rhema Word of God. His spoken Word—his Rhema Word—speaks directly to you about you and your current circumstances. It's personal.

Have you ever read a particular verse in the Bible or heard words in a song or read a quote card, or listened to a sermon that seemed as though it was speaking directly to you? When you are a believer in Christ and ask God to help you, he often speaks to you by giving a Rhema Word, a word he is speaking directly to you. These words come in different forms. For instance, when you read a passage in the Bible or hear a phrase in a song that seems to apply directly to you that day or that moment, it is often a Rhema Word, a spoken word directly from God to you. It is a word that has the power to make a difference in your soul—your mind, heart, and free will. It has the power to demolish the lies of the Enemy, break down strongholds, and expose your deep-seated false core beliefs.

Once the door from your spirit to your soul is unlocked, the Holy Spirit will give you the power to break free. The Rhema Word of God will be revealed to you. His spoken Word is more than words written on a page. They are living words that apply directly to you and your life circumstances. However, this Rhema Word can initiate a battle within your soul. Your heart and your mind wage war against each other. They battle over choosing the truth of God or the lies of the Enemy. When you merge the knowledge of God's Word with his undefiled truth by the power source given to you through the Holy Spirit, you are then equipped to win this battle in your mind. You have the supernatural ability to challenge and overthrow the devil's schemes and lies.

Drinking the cup of challenging, difficult, or even devastating circumstances is never something anyone wants to do. When you find yourself facing an unwanted or bitter cup, be assured there is a loving

God who will help you follow in the footsteps of his Son, Jesus, when you say what he said that day in the garden: "Nevertheless, not my will, but yours" (Luke 22:42 ESV). Through the death and resurrection and ascension of Christ, you have been given the opportunity to be saved by his grace. Once you receive Christ into your life, you are given supernatural power through the Holy Spirit to drink life's bitter cup, knowing God is with you and has a bigger plan. He will give you peace and comfort. He will equip you with all you need to fight off the Enemy's lies and will open your eyes to look beyond what is in front of you to see the bigger picture and know there is hope for your future.

Whether you are faced with doubt, despair, shame, fear, or sorrow, you have everything it takes to walk courageously into the unknown, holding on tight to the God who knows and loves you. There are tools you can use to understand, change, and eliminate fearful thinking, warped perceptions, strongholds, and false core beliefs. When you find yourself spinning and asking God why, remember asking why won't stop the spin. Instead of asking why, lean into the character and nature of who God is—he is faithful, loving, merciful, holy, and sovereign. He sees the bigger picture. If you are doubting God's ability to deliver you from your pain, remember he often delivers those he loves *through* their circumstances, not directly *out* of them. While on the journey of being delivered through, he will bring a complete transformation to your heart and mind. If you feel as though you are not good enough or do not deserve to receive the love of God, those feelings are rooted in a lie of shame. Satan wants you to believe you are damaged goods unworthy of grace and redemption. Discovering the root of your faulty beliefs will lead you down a path to emotional healing and spiritual freedom. Satan wants you to fear the outcome of your circumstance and to lose faith in God's ability to intervene. He knows if he can get your eyes off

Jesus and onto your circumstance, fear will take over and cause you to fall deeper into despair. Keeping your eyes on Jesus will give you the courage and strength to rise above the storm. Your hope is in him and him alone. When your emotions and feelings try to take over, be like David and sit with them. Your feelings are not good or bad; they just are. Acknowledge and validate them even if they seem out of range. Once you have owned all of your feelings, take action to change your thoughts and perceptions that perpetuate your unwanted feelings. With Jesus by your side, you can get through your circumstance, whatever it is, and have the courage to drink the cup you have been served. The journey is rarely easy, but God is continually with you, giving you enough even if it means only enough for one minute at a time—but it is always enough.

"And after you have suffered a little while, the God of all grace, who has called you to his eternal glory in Christ, will himself restore, confirm, strengthen and establish you." 1 Peter 5:10.

Acknowledgments

*A*t one time, I had given up on this work. The dream had died. Then the phone rang and a woman said these words to me: "I believe in your writing. You have a gift." Jennifer Strickland gave me the confidence to believe again. She took me under her wing, and taught me how to write. When the process seemed too daunting, she coached me to push through the pain to give birth to the message you now hold in your hands. Thank you, Jennifer, for believing in me. Your support gave me the courage to pick up my pen and write again.

I want to thank my dearest friend, Lisa Nance, whose high-level thinking brought clarity when I got lost in the messiness. You are the queen of the metaphor. You untangled my analogies piece by piece like a ball of yarn and helped me stitch them together into the tapestry of this book. You stood alongside me this entire journey and became my biggest cheerleader. Whenever I was discouraged or doubted my ability to finish a thought, you listened and gave me the words of encouragement I needed to move forward. I also want to thank you for having the courage to allow me to share your story.

My son, Christopher: Your willingness to sit with me and work through these concepts means so much to me as your mom. As a doctoral candidate studying the behavior and neuro-circuitry of emotional loss, your contribution to the areas of perception and cognitive behavioral therapy was invaluable. Thank you for taking the time to read, critique, and design my illustrations. Your input has helped shape the content of this book.

My sweet daughter Tori, who has walked through so much: Your courage to open your soul and share your journey through the depths of depression illuminated for me the value of radically accepting your feelings. Your personal experience with dialectical behavior therapy was vital to this book. I am so proud of you. Never forget you are more than a conqueror. I could not have mastered the chapter on feelings without your contributions and insight. Thank you.

Maddie: You are my ray of sunshine. Your creative brilliance has given life to this book. Thank you for holding my hand through the complexities of social media and building a beautiful platform for me to reach the people who need this message most.

Marcy Jiminez: Publishing this book would not have been possible without you. When I shared with you my vision, you told me I should ask God for what I needed and to have faith he would provide. You have shown me what having strong faith looks like. You are such an inspiration to me, and your friendship is a precious gift. Thank you, Marcy, for believing in and supporting me throughout this entire process.

Dad: Thank you for teaching me the concepts of the body, soul, and spirit. These truths are at the heart of this book. You have left me a priceless legacy of what it truly means to love God and trust in him through all life's ups and downs.

Deana Morgan: You saw the thoroughbred in me before I could run. You have always believed in me, even when I did not believe in myself. Thank you for faithfully standing beside me, elevating me and calling out my purpose.

Rachelle Fletcher: I would not be here today writing these words had you not given my first chapter to Jennifer. Having been friends since we were young teenagers, we've been on a journey to fulfill what we believed were our destinies. That night at the Gathering, I was so broken. Then you sang the song "New Wine" and the Holy Spirit showed me: *In the crushing, he will pour out new wine.* This book is that wine.

Acknowledgments

It is with deep emotion that I acknowledge the one person who has stood alongside me, mentoring and loving me since I was a young teenager. Joy Headley has seen it all. She has walked with me through every mountaintop and valley experience. She has prayed with me during times of deep sorrow and counseled me through the blinding sprays and twisted turns of the unexpected. Joy taught me to always surrender my heart and will to God and trust in him. Because of her influence, I was able to grow deep spiritual roots that enabled me to drink the cup I was served and look beyond my pain to see the beauty that surrounded me.

*C*onnie Hagen is an ordained minister through Christ for the Nation's Institute in Dallas, Texas. For ten years, she was a private-practice licensed professional counselor who worked with women recovering from trauma. Through her ministry, she has cultivated a unique ability to connect with women who have experienced suffering, loss, brokenness, grief, and shame.

Connie received her undergraduate degree in psychology from Evangel University as well as her master's of education degree in marriage and family counseling from the University of North Texas. She obtained her LPC license and specialized in post-traumatic stress disorder, depression, and anxiety in women.

In 2004, she made the decision to devote herself to her growing family— Christopher, Tori, Maddie, and her husband, Jeff. Her husband left a large OB/GYN Medical Group in the DFW area to establish a private practice in the small town of Bastrop, Texas. For the next fifteen years, she dedicated herself to raising her children and managing her husband's medical practice. Their shared vision to provide medical care to the underserved and economically disadvantaged was a natural progression of Connie's passion to serve women in need.

She currently serves as director of the women's ministry at her local church, where she uses her gifts of teaching and public speaking on a regular basis.

IF YOU ENJOYED THIS BOOK,
PLEASE CONSIDER SHARING IT WITH OTHERS.

Recommend this book personally to friends and family, as well as to those in your small group, book club, workplace, and classes.

Mention the book in a blog post or on Twitter, or upload a photo of the cover with your positive review to Instagram, Facebook, and Pinterest.

Connect with the author on Facebook to express your appreciation for the book's message and, perhaps, how it had a positive effect on your life.

Order a copy of the book for someone you know who would be challenged and encouraged by its message.

Look for the book on Amazon.com and leave a positive review.

And visit us to see the many other books, products, and publishing services we offer.

CreativeEnterprisesStudio.com

1507 SHIRLEY WAY, SUITE A
BEDFORD, TX 76022-6737
ACREATIVESHOP@AOL.COM